DATE

D0440570

A THEORY OF PERSONALITY

The Psychology of Personal Constructs

ЛЛЛЛЛЛЛЛЛЛЛЛЛЛЛЛЛЛЛЛЛЛЛЛ

LIBRARY
COLLEGE of the REDWOODS
EUREKA
7351 Tompkins Hill Road
Eureka, California 95501

BF 698 .K39
Kelly, George, 1905-1967.
A theory of personality

A THEORY
OF
PERSONALITY

The Psychology of Personal Constructs

By GEORGE A. KELLY, *Ph.D.*

W · W · NORTON & COMPANY

New York · London

Copyright © 1963 and 1955 by George A. Kelly

First published in Norton paperback 1963

ALL RIGHTS RESERVED

W. W. Norton & Company, Inc.
500 Fifth Avenue, New York, N.Y. 10110
www.wwnorton.com

W. W. Norton & Company Ltd.
Castle House, 75/76 Wells Street, London W1T 3QT

Printed in the United States of America

8 9 0

ISBN: 978-0-393-00152-5

Contents

To a lot of people I know, and some I don't, most of whom I like, and some I don't, but acquaintances or strangers, friends or scoundrels, I must confess I am indebted to them all.

Introduction

Several years ago, W. W. Norton published *The Psychology of Personal Constructs*, a two volume, twenty-year collection of impacted ideas about a new theory of personality and its application in a clinical setting. Presumably it was the sort of thing more likely to be purchased than read. At least *I* would have presumed so. Yet there do appear to have been some readers, and as a result Norton recently proposed publication of the present edition, an excerpt comprising the first three chapters of Volume 1. Chapter one invites attention to some philosophical assumptions without which the notion of personal constructs would be little more than another outcropping of nineteenth-century phenomenology. Chapter two consists of a somewhat formal and loosely linked series of abstract theoretical statements. The concluding chapter offers a descriptive elaboration of the theory intended to help make the whole business come alive. Omitted from this volume is the scientific methodology of personal construct theory, its mathematical construction of psychological space, its more humanistic approaches to man as a person, and its multifaceted ways of coping with human distress.

As with the original edition of this work, it is only fair to warn the reader that he will find missing many of the familiar landmarks of psychology theory. In this new way of thinking about psychology, there is no *learning*, no *motivation*, no *emotion*, no *cognition*, no *stimulus*, no *response*, no *ego*, no *unconscious*, no *need*, no *reinforcement*, no *drive*. It is not only that these terms are abandoned; what is more important, the concepts themselves evaporate. If the reader starts murmuring such words to himself, he can be sure he has lost the scent. All of this will make for periods of strange and perhaps uncomfortable reading; yet, inevitably, a different approach calls for a different lexicon.

It may be unreasonable, merely on the basis of a few pages of academic prose, to ask a reader to reconsider his notions of why man does what he does. Yet that is the burden of this invitation. To respond, one should prepare himself as best he can to surmount some formidable barriers — barriers raised high by more than two thousand years of constructive thought and held rigidly in place by the only languages we speak aloud.

What is more, this may come as a frightening invitation to those who have entrusted themselves wholly to external things which they assume are beyond reexamination. Yet man is always free to reconstrue what he may not deny. This should be a source of comfort, not of dismay. Moreover, to give oneself over to a reconsideration of his views is not necessarily to abandon the old and embrace the new, nor does a man always need to suppress what is novel in order to conserve what is familiar.

But here, here! We are getting much too far ahead of ourselves. This is what the book, not the preface, is supposed to say.

G. A. K.

A THEORY OF PERSONALITY

The Psychology of Personal Constructs

Chapter One

Constructive Alternativism

ЛЛЛЛЛЛЛЛЛЛЛЛЛЛЛЛЛЛЛЛЛЛЛЛЛЛЛЛЛЛЛЛ

IN THIS chapter, instead of starting immediately with a statement of our theoretical position, we reach back to uncover some of its philosophical roots. Constructive alternativism not only underlies our theory, but it is also an explicit and recurrent theme throughout our later discussion of psychotherapeutic techniques.

A. Points of Departure

1. PERSPECTIVES ON MAN

This theory of personality actually started with the combination of two simple notions: first, that man might be better understood if he were viewed in the perspective of the centuries rather than in the flicker of passing moments; and second, that each man contemplates in his own personal way the stream of events upon which he finds himself so swiftly borne. Perhaps within this interplay of the durable and the ephemeral we may discover ever more hopeful ways in which the individual man can restructure his life. The idea seems worth pursuing.

Neither the notion of man's march through the centuries nor that of his personally biased nature is especially new. The successive literature of the Old Testament portrays a well-known epic story of man's progress. Nor has the stream of the individual man's life escaped the attention of curious students. The highly articulate William James was fascinated by the currents and eddies in the stream of consciousness. The inarticulate Adolph Meyer urged his students to draw a time line through the facts of their patients' lives. The sensitive Sigmund Freud waded into the headwaters of the stream in a search for the underground springs which fed it. And the impulsive Henri Bergson jumped from the bank into the current and, as he was carried along, speculated that mind could be used as a yardstick for measuring time. As for personal ways of looking at things: Solomon, in writing about the worried man, said, "As he thinketh in his heart, so is he." And Shelley once wrote, "The mind becomes that which it contemplates." John Locke, struck by the unique imperceptiveness of each of his friends during an evening's discussion, sat down to write the *Essay Concerning Human Understanding* before retiring for the night — a task which, incidentally, he did not finish until twenty years later.

The long-range view of man leads us to turn our attention toward those factors appearing to account for his progress rather than those betraying his impulses. To a large degree — though not entirely — the blueprint of human progress has been given the label of "science." Let us then, instead of occupying ourselves with *man-the-biological-organism* or *man-the-lucky-guy*, have a look at *man-the-scientist*.

At this point we depart again from the usual manner of looking at things. When we speak of *man-the-scientist* we are speaking of all mankind and not merely a particular class of men who have publicly attained the stature of "scientists." We are speaking of all mankind in its scientist-like aspects, rather than all mankind in its biological aspects or all mankind in its appetitive aspects. Moreover, we are speaking of aspects of mankind rather than collections of men. Thus the notion of *man-the-scientist* is a particular abstraction of all mankind and not a concrete classification of particular men.

Such an abstraction of the nature of man is not altogether new. The Reformation called attention to the priesthood of all men in contrast to the concretistic classification of certain men only as priests. The democratic political inventions of the eighteenth and nineteenth centuries hinged on the notion of the inherent rulership of all men in contrast to the older notion of a concrete class of rulers. In a similar fashion we may replace the concretistic notion of scientists being set apart from nonscientists and, like the reformists who insisted that every man is his own priest, propose that every man is, in his own particular way, a scientist.

Let us see what it would mean to construe man in his scientist-like aspect. What is it that is supposed to characterize the motivation of the scientist? It is customary to say that *the scientist's ultimate aim is to predict and control.* This is a summary statement that psychologists frequently like to quote in characterizing their own aspirations. Yet, curiously enough, psychologists rarely credit the human subjects in their experiments with having similar aspirations. It is as though the psychologist were saying to himself, "I, being a *psychologist,* and therefore a *scientist,* am performing this experiment in order to improve the prediction and control of certain human phenomena; but my subject, being merely a human organism, is obviously propelled by inexorable drives welling up within him, or else he is in gluttonous pursuit of sustenance and shelter."

Now what would happen if we were to reopen the question of human motivation and use our long-range view of man to infer just what it is that sets the course of his endeavor? Would we see his centuried progress in terms of appetites, tissue needs, or sex impulses? Or might he, in this perspective, show a massive drift of quite a different sort? Might not the individual man, each in his own personal way, assume more of the stature of a scientist, ever seeking to predict and control the course of events with which he is involved? Would he not have his theories, test his hypotheses, and weigh his experimental evidence? And, if so, might not the differences between the personal viewpoints of different men correspond to the differences between the theoretical points of view of different scientists?

Here is an intriguing idea. It stems from an attempt to consolidate the viewpoints of the clinician, the historian, the scientist, and the philosopher. But where does it lead? For considerable time now some of us have been attempting to discover the answer to this question. The present manuscript is a report of what has appeared on our horizons thus far.

2. WHAT KIND OF UNIVERSE?

All thinking is based, in part, on prior convictions. A complete philosophical or scientific system attempts to make all these prior convictions explicit. That is a large order, and there are few, if any, writers who can actually fill it. While we have no intention of trying to build a complete system at this point, it does seem to be incumbent upon us to attempt to be explicit about some of our more important prior convictions. The first of these convictions has to do with the kind of universe we envision.

We presume that the universe is really existing and that man is gradually coming to understand it. By taking this position we attempt to make clear from the outset that it is a real world we shall be talking about, not a world composed solely of the flitting shadows of people's thoughts. But we should like, furthermore, to make clear our conviction that people's thoughts also really exist, though the correspondence between what people really think exists and what really does exist is a continually changing one.

The universe that we presume exists has another important characteristic: it is integral. By that we mean it functions as a single unit with all its imaginable parts having an exact relationship to each other. This may, at first, seem a little implausible, since ordinarily it would appear that there is a closer relationship between the motion of my fingers and the action of the typewriter keys than there is, say, between either of them and the price of yak milk in Tibet. But we believe that, in the long run, all of these events — the motion of my fingers, the action of the keys, and the price of yak milk — are interlocked. It is only within a limited section of the universe, that part we call earth and that span of time we recognize as our present eon, that two of these necessarily seem more closely related to each other than either of them is to the third. A simple way of saying this is to state that *time provides the ultimate bond in all relationships.*

We can express the same idea through extrapolation from a well-known mathematical relationship. Consider the coefficient of correlation between two variables. If that coefficient is anything but zero and if it expresses a linear relationship, then an infinite increase in the variance of one of the variables will cause the coefficient to approach unity as a limit. The magnitude of the coefficient of correlation is therefore directly proportional to the breadth of perspective in which we envision the variables whose relationship it expresses. This is basically true of all relationships within our universe.

Another important prior conviction is that the universe can be measured along a dimension of time. This is a way of saying that the universe is continually changing with respect to itself. Since time is the one dimension which must always be considered if we are to contemplate change, we have chosen this particular way of saying that within our universe something is always going on. In fact, that is the way the universe exists; it exists by happening. Actually we tried to convey the same notion when we said in an earlier paragraph that the universe is really *existing*. Indeed, every day and all day it goes about its business of existing. It is hard to imagine what the world would be like if it just sat there and did nothing. Philosophers used to try to contemplate such a world, but, somehow, they never got very far with it.

The three prior convictions about the universe that we have emphasized in this section are that it is real and not a figment of our imginations, that it all works together like clockwork, and that it is something that is going on all the time and not something that merely stays put.

3. WHAT IS LIFE?

There are some parts of the universe which make a good deal of sense even when they are not viewed in the perspective of time. But there are other parts which make sense only when they are plotted along a time line. Life is one of the latter. This is a point about which we shall have a great deal to say later when we talk about ways to reconstruct personal lives. Whether it be the research-minded psychologist or the frantic client in the psychological clinic, life has to be seen in the perspective of time if it is to make any sense at all.

But life, to our way of thinking, is more than mere change. It involves an interesting relationship between parts of our universe wherein one part, the living creature, is able to bring himself around to represent another part, his environment. Sometimes it is said that the living thing is "sensitive," in contrast to the nonliving thing, or that he is capable of "reaction." This is roughly the same distinctive characteristic of life that we envision. But we like our formulation better because *it emphasizes the creative capacity of the living thing to represent the environment, not merely to respond to it.* Because he can represent his environment, he can place alternative constructions upon it and, indeed, do something about it if it doesn't suit him. To the living creature, then, the universe is real, but it is not inexorable unless he chooses to construe it that way.

In emphasizing the prior conviction that life involves the representation or construction of reality, we should not imply that life is not itself real. Sometimes scientists, particularly those who are engrossed in the study of physical systems, take the stand that psychological events are not true phenomena but are rather epiphenomena, or merely the unreliable shadows of real events. This position is not ours. A person may misrepresent a real phenomenon, such as his income or his ills, and yet his misrepresentation will itself be entirely real. This applies even to the badly deluded patient: what he perceives may not exist, but his perception does. Moreover, his fictitious perception will often turn out to be a grossly distorted construction of something which actually does exist. Any living creature, together with his perceptions, is a part of the real world; he is not merely a near-sighted bystander to the goings-on of the real world.

Life, then, to our way of thinking, is characterized by its essential measurability in the dimension of time and its capacity to represent other forms of reality, while still retaining its own form of reality.

4. CONSTRUCTION SYSTEMS

Man looks at his world through transparent patterns or templets which he creates and then attempts to fit over the realities of which the world is composed. The fit is not always very good. Yet without such patterns the world appears to be such an undifferentiated homogeneity that man is unable to make any sense out of it. Even a poor fit is more helpful to him than nothing at all.

Let us give the name *constructs* to these patterns that are tentatively tried on for size. They are ways of construing the world. They are what enables man, and lower animals too, to chart a course of behavior, explicitly formulated or implicitly acted out, verbally expressed or utterly inarticulate, consistent with other courses of behavior or inconsistent with them, intellectually reasoned or vegetatively sensed.

In general man seeks to improve his constructs by increasing his repertory, by altering them to provide better fits, and by subsuming them with superordinate constructs or systems. In seeking improvement he is repeatedly halted by the damage to the system that apparently will result from the alteration of a subordinate construct. Frequently his personal investment in the larger system, or his personal dependence upon it, is so great that he will forego the adoption of a more precise construct in the substructure. It may take a major act of psychotherapy or experience to get him to adjust his construction system to the point where the new and more precise construct can be incorporated.

Those construction systems which can be communicated can be widely shared. The last half century has shown much progress in the development of ways of making personal constructs and construction systems more communicable. We have developed a scientific psychological vocabulary. A better way of saying this is that our public construction systems for understanding other people's personal constructs are becoming more precise and more comprehensive.

Certain widely shared or public construction systems are designed primarily to fit special fields or realms of facts. When one limits the realm of facts, it is possible to develop a detailed system without worrying about the inconsistencies in the system which certain peripheral facts would reveal. We limit the *realm* and try to ignore, for the time being, the intransigent facts just outside the borders of that *realm*. For example, it has long been customary and convenient to distinguish between "mental" and "physical" facts. These are two artificially distinguished realms, to which two types of construction systems are respectively fitted: the psychological construction system and the natural-science group of construction systems. It is becoming increasingly clear, however, that we have on our hands two alternative construction systems, which can both be applied profitably to an ever increasing body of the same facts. The realms overlap.

Consider more specifically the realms of psychology and physiology. These realms have been given tentative boundaries based upon the presumed ranges of convenience of the psychological and the physiological construction systems, respectively. But many of the same facts can be construed within either system. Are those facts "psychological facts" or are they "physiological facts"? Where do they really belong? Who gets possession of them, the psychologist or the physiologist? While this may seem like a silly question, one has only to sit in certain interdisciplinary staff conferences to see it arise in the discussions between people of different professional guilds. Some individuals can get badly worked up over the protection of their exclusive rights to construe particular facts.

The answer is, of course, that the events upon which facts are based hold no institutional loyalties. They are in the public domain. The same event may be construed simultaneously and profitably within various disciplinary systems — physics, physiology, political science, or psychology.

No one has yet proved himself wise enough to propound a universal system of constructs. We can safely assume that it will be a long time before a satisfactorily unified system will be proposed. For the time being we shall have to content ourselves with a series of miniature systems, each with its own realm or limited range of convenience. As long as we continue to use such a disjointed combination of miniature systems we shall have to be careful to apply each system abstractly rather than concretively. For example, instead of saying that a certain event is a "psychological event and therefore not a physiological event," we must be careful to recognize that any event may be viewed either in its psychological or in its physiological aspects. A further idea that we must keep straight is that the physiologically constructed facts about that event are the offspring of the physiological system within which they emerge and have meaning, and that a psychological system is not obliged to account for them.

It is also important that we continue to recognize the limited ranges of convenience of our miniature systems. It is always tempting, once a miniature system has proved itself useful within a limited range of convenience, to try to extend its range of convenience. For example, in the field of psychology we have seen Hull's mathematico-deductive theory of rote learning extended to the realm of problem solving or even to the realm of personality. Freud's psychoanalysis started out as a psychotherapeutic technique but was progressively enlarged into a personality system and, by some, into a religio-philosophical system. This kind of inflation of miniature systems is not necessarily a bad thing, but it does cause trouble when one fails to recognize that what is reasonably true within a limited range is not necessarily quite so true outside that range.

Any psychological system is likely to have a limited range of convenience. In fact, psychological systems may, for some time to come, have to get along with more limited ranges of convenience than psychologists would like. The system or theory which we are about to expound and explore has a limited range of convenience, its range being restricted, as far as we can see at this moment, to human personality and, more particularly, to problems of interpersonal relationships.

Not only do systems, psychological and otherwise, tend to have limited ranges of convenience, but they also have foci of convenience. There are points within its realm of events where a system or a theory tends to work best. Usually these are the points which the author had in mind when he devised the system. For example, our own theory, we believe, tends to have its focus of convenience in the area of human readjustment to stress. Thus it should prove most useful to the psychotherapist because we were thinking primarily of the problems of psychotherapy when we formulated it.

In this section we hoped to make clear our conviction that man creates his own ways of seeing the world in which he lives; the world does not create them for him. He builds constructs and tries them on for size. His constructs are sometimes organized into systems, groups of constructs which embody subordinate and superordinate relationships. The same events can often be viewed in the light of two or more systems. Yet the events do not belong to any system. Moreover, man's practical systems have particular foci and limited ranges of convenience.

5. CONSTRUCTS AS GROUNDS FOR PREDICTIONS

We started out with two notions: (1) that, viewed in the perspective of the centuries, man might be seen as an incipient scientist, and (2) that each individual man formulates in his own way constructs through which he views the world of events. As a scientist, man seeks to predict, and thus control, the course of events. It follows, then, that the constructs which he formulates are intended to aid him in his predictive efforts.

We have not yet tried to be very explicit about what a construct is. That undertaking is reserved for a later chapter. But we have already said enough to indicate that we consider a construct to be a representation of the universe, a representation erected by a living creature and then tested against the reality of that universe. Since the universe is essentially a course of events, the testing of a construct is a testing against subsequent events. In other words, a construct is tested in terms of its predictive efficiency.

Actually the testing of a construct in terms of its predictive efficiency may turn out to be a somewhat redundant affair. A man construes his neighbor's behavior as hostile. By that he means that his neighbor, given the proper opportunity, will do him harm. He tries out his construction of his neighbor's attitude by throwing rocks at his neighbor's dog. His neighbor responds with an angry rebuke. The man may then believe that he has validated his construction of his neighbor as a hostile person.

The man's construction of his neighbor as a hostile person may appear to be "validated" by another kind of fallacy. The man reasons, "If my neighbor is hostile, he will be eager to know when I get into trouble, when I am ill, or when I am in any way vulnerable. I will watch to see if this isn't so." The next morning the man meets his neighbor and is greeted with the conventional, "How are you?" Sure enough, the neighbor is doing just what was predicted of a hostile person!

Just as constructs are used to forecast events, so they must also be used to assess the accuracy of the forecast, after the events have occurred. Man would be hopelessly bogged down in his biases if it were not for the fact that he can usually assess the outcomes of his predictions at a different level of construction from that at which he originally makes them. A man bets that a horse will win a certain race because it is black and he has recently won with a black hand at poker. When the race results are in, however, he is likely to construe the announced decision of the judges as being more palpable evidence of the horse's performance in the race than is the horse's color.

When constructs are used to predict immediate happenings, they become more susceptible to change or revision. The validational evidence is quickly available. If they are used solely to predict an event in the remote future, such as life after death or the end of the world, they are not likely to be so open to revision. Besides, most people are in no hurry to collect validational evidence in such matters.

A good scientist tries to bring his constructs up for test as soon as possible. But he tries them out initially in test-tube proportions. If hazards appear to be great, he will first seek some indirect evidence on the probable outcome of his trials. This straightforward testing of constructs is one of the features of the experimental method in modern science. It also characterizes any alert person.

But there are times when a person hesitates to experiment because he dreads the outcome. He may fear that the conclusion of the experiment will place him in an ambiguous position where he will no longer be able to predict and control. He does not want to be caught with his constructs down. He may even keep his constructs strictly to himself lest he be trapped into testing them prematurely. This reluctance either to express or to test one's constructs is, of course, one of the practical problems which confront the psychotherapist in dealing with his client. We shall have more to say about these issues later.

Constructs are used for predictions of things to come, and the world keeps rolling along and revealing these predictions to be either correct or misleading. This fact provides the basis for revision of constructs and, eventually, of whole construction systems. If it were a static world that we lived in, our thinking about it might be static too. But new things keep happening and our predictions keep turning out in expected or unexpected ways. Each day's experience calls for the consolidation of some aspects of our outlook, revision of some, and outright abandonment of others.

What we have said about the experience of the individual man holds true also for the scientist. A scientist formulates a theory — a body of constructs with a focus and a range of convenience. If he is a good scientist, he immediately starts putting it to test. It is almost certain that, as soon as he starts testing, he will also have to start changing it in the light of the outcomes. Any theory, then, tends to be transient. And the more practical it is and the more useful it appears to be, the more vulnerable it is to new evidence. Our own theory, particularly if it proves to be practical, will also have to be considered expendable in the light of tomorrow's outlooks and discoveries. At best it is an ad interim theory.

B. *The Philosophical Position*
6. STATEMENT OF CONSTRUCTIVE ALTERNATIVISM

Enough has already been said to make clear our position that there are various ways in which the world is construed. Some of them are undoubtedly better than others. They are better from our human point of view because they support more precise and more accurate predictions about more events. No one has yet devised a set of constructs which will predict everything down to the last tiny flutter of a hummingbird's wing; we think it will be an infinitely long time before anyone does. Since an absolute construction of the universe is not feasible, we shall have to be content with a series of successive approximations to it. These successive approximations can, in turn, be tested piecemeal for their predictive efficiency. Essentially this means that all of our interpretations of the universe can gradually be scientifically evaluated if we are persistent and keep on learning from our mistakes.

We assume that all of our present interpretations of the universe are subject to revision or replacement. This is a basic statement which has a bearing upon almost everything that we shall have to say later. We take the stand that there are always some alternative constructions available to choose among in dealing with the world. No one needs to paint himself into a corner; no one needs to be completely hemmed in by circumstances; no one needs to be the victim of his biography. We call this philosophical position *constructive alternativism.*

We have now said enough about the testing of constructs to indicate that it is not a matter of indifference which of a set of alternative constructions one chooses to impose upon his world. Constructs cannot be tossed about willy-nilly without a person's getting into difficulty. While there are always alternative constructions available, some of them are definitely poor implements. The yardstick to use is the specific predictive efficiency of each alternative construct and the over-all predictive efficiency of the system of which it would, if adopted, become a part.

7. PHILOSOPHY OR PSYCHOLOGY?

Scholars customarily distinguish sharply between the forms of thought and the actual thinking behavior of people. The study of the former is classified under *philosophy* — or more particularly, *logic* — while the latter is considered to be *psychology.*

But we have taken the basic view that whatever is characteristic of thought is descriptive of the thinker; that the essentials of scientific curiosity must underlie human curiosity in general. If we examine a person's philosophy closely, we find ourselves staring at the person himself. If we reach an understanding of how a person behaves, we discover it in the manner in which he represents his circumstances to himself.

A person is not necessarily articulate about the constructions he places upon his world. Some of his constructions are not symbolized by words; he can express them only in pantomime. Even the elements which are construed may have no verbal handles by which they can be manipulated and the person finds himself responding to them with speechless impulse. Thus, in studying the psychology of man-the-philosopher, we must take into account his subverbal patterns of representation and construction.

What we are proposing is neither a conventional philosophy nor a conventional psychology. As a philosophy it is rooted in the psychological observation of man. As a psychology it is concerned with the philosophical outlooks of individual man. Upon this framework we propose to erect a limited psychological theory.

8. RELATION TO PHILOSOPHICAL SYSTEMS

Constructive alternativism represents a philosophical point of view, but we have no intention of trying to elaborate it into a complete philosophical system. It may, however, be useful to attempt to plot its position roughly with respect to some of the types of philosophical systems with which scholars are familiar.

Realm-wise, constructive alternativism falls within that area of epistemology which is sometimes called *gnosiology* — the "systematic analysis of the conceptions employed by ordinary and scientific thought in interpreting the world, and including an investigation of the art of knowledge, or the nature of knowledge as such." The emphasis upon the constructs through which the world is scanned suggests *positivism*, although most of the criticisms that are leveled at Comte are not applicable here.

Comte's positivism is too often deprecated in terms of some of his concrete proposals rather than evaluated in terms of the abstract features of the system.

Our emphasis upon the testing of constructs implies our reliance upon the principles of *empiricism* and, more particularly, *pragmatic logic.* In this respect we are in the tradition of present-day American psychology. But, because we recognize that man approaches his world through construing it, we are, in a measure, *rationalistic.* Moreover, since we insist that man can erect his own alternative approaches to reality, we are out of line with traditional *realism,* which insists that he is always the victim of his circumstances.

Ontologically, our position is identifiable as a form of *monism,* although, in view of the many complex varieties of ontology, the differentiation of its monistic from its pluralistic aspects is hardly worth the effort. If it is a monism, it is a *substantival* monism that we are talking about; yet it is *neutral,* and, like Spinoza, we are prepared to apply *attributive pluralism* to the substance whenever our purposes might be served thereby.

Two classical issues remain to be discussed: *determinism vs. free will,* and *phenomenology.* Since both problems have to do with our design specifications for a theory of personality, we reserve the discussion of them for the next division of this chapter.

9. THE REALM OF PSYCHOLOGY

The realm of psychology is limited practically to that which can be spanned by whatever psychological theory we happen to be using at the moment. The theory's range of convenience is what determines the boundaries of the discipline. A range of convenience is that expanse of the real world over which a given system or theory provides useful coverage. Those features of the universe which do not fit neatly into the system are left out of the psychological realm for the time being. If we are reasonably good psychologists, there should still be enough of the universe remaining for us to make ourselves useful by structuring it. Later, if our theoretical reasoning is extended, further areas may fall within our ken.

There are, of course, various psychological construction systems. These systems differ primarily because the people who developed them were focusing their attention upon somewhat different events. Psychological systems have not only ranges of convenience but also characteristic foci of convenience: points at which they are particularly applicable. Thus stimulus-response theories are particularly convenient at the focal point of animal learning, field theories at the focal point of human perception, and psychoanalytic theories at the focal point of human neurosis.

There is no clear criterion by which a theory can be labeled "psychological," and not "physiological" or "sociological." There is much interrelationship. The stimulus-response theories in psychology bear a close family resemblance to the interaction theories of physiology. There are field theories in physiology which resemble the psychology of Gestalt. Whether a theory is called "psychological," "physiological," or "sociological" probably depends upon its original focus of convenience.

10. THE FUNCTION OF A THEORY

A theory may be considered as a way of binding together a multitude of facts so that one may comprehend them all at once. When the theory enables us to make reasonably precise predictions, one may call it scientific. If its predictions are so elastic that a wide variety of conceivable events can be construed as corroborative, the theory fails to meet the highest standards of science.

A theory need not be highly scientific in order to be useful. All of us order the daily events of our lives by constructions that are somewhat elastic. Under these constructions our anticipations of daily events, while not scientifically precise, nevertheless surround our lives with an aura of meaning. Because life does not seem wholly capricious we are prepared by our personal construction systems to take each day's new experience in our stride.

But this is not all. A theory provides a basis for an active approach to life, not merely a comfortable armchair from which to contemplate its vicissitudes with detached complaisance. Mankind need not be a throng of stony-faced spectators witnessing the pageant of creation. Men can play active roles in the shaping of events. How they can be free to do this and still themselves be construed as lawful beings is a basic issue in any psychological theory.

The answer lies, first of all, in our recognition of the essentially active nature of our universe. The world is not an abandoned monument. It is an event of tremendous proportions, the conclusion of which is not yet apparent. The theories that men employ to construe this event are themselves incidents in the mammoth procession. The truths the theories attempt to fix are successive approximations to the larger scheme of things which slowly they help to unfold. Thus a theory is a tentative expression of what man has seen as a regular pattern in the surging events of life. But the theory, being itself an event, can in turn be subsumed by another theory, or by a superordinate part of itself, and that in turn can be subsumed by another. A theory is thus bound only by the construction system of which it is understood to be a part — and, of course, the binding is only temporary, lasting only as long as that particular superordinate system is employed.

11. DETERMINISM AND MAN'S FREE WILL

A theory binds or determines the events which are subordinated to it. It is not determined by the events themselves; it is determined by the superordinating point of view of the theorist. Yet it must conform to events in order to predict them. The number of alternative ways of conforming are, as far as we know, infinite, but discriminable from the infinite number of ways which do not conform.

A person is to cut a pie. There is an infinite number of ways of going about it, all of which may be relevant to the task. If the pie is frozen, some of the usual ways of cutting the pie may not work — but there is still an infinite number of ways of going about it. But suppose the pie is on the table and there is company present. Certain limiting expectations have been set up

about how a meal is to be served. The pie is construed as part
of the meal. There are also certain conventions about serving
wedge-shaped slices with the point always turned toward the
diner. If one accepts all the usual superordinating constructions
of the situation, he may, indeed, find his course of behavior determined and very little latitude left to him. He is not the victim of the pie, but of his notions of etiquette under which the
pie cutting has been subsumed.

But suppose the pie makes him sick. Is he not then a victim
of circumstances? We might then ask why he ate it in the first
place. We could even suggest that his illness need not rob him
of his freedom. The illness may even increase his scope of action, as many children and hypochondriacs have discovered.

The relation established by a construct or a construction system over its subordinate elements is deterministic. In this sense
the tendency to subordinate constitutes determinism. The natural events themselves do not subordinate our constructions of
them; we can look at them in any way we like. But, of course,
if we wish to predict natural events accurately, we need to
erect some kind of construction which will serve the purpose.
But the events do not come around and tell us how to do the job
— they just go about their business of being themselves. The
structure we erect is what rules us.

Actually there are two forms of determinism which concern
us. The one is the determinism which is the essential feature of
any organized construction system — the control of superordinate constructs over subordinate elements. The second is implied
in our notion of an integral universe. The universe as it flows
along is not essentially divided into independent events like cars
on a railroad train. It is an essential continuity. Because of this
continuity we may consider that there is determinism operating
between antecedent and subsequent events. This is the continuity which is assumed in the so-called First Postulate of
Logic, the Postulate of Cosmic Connectedness.

But the second kind of determinism is, to our way of thinking, relatively unimportant. The universe flows on and on.
While one may abstract certain repetitive features in its course,

it never actually doubles back on itself. Matters would become enormously confused if it ever did. (The very idea of a universe that doubled back on itself is highly amusing and might even have some relativistic significance for a cosmic theorist.) Since we assume that the universe does not double back on itself, any sequence of events is the only sequence of its exact identical sort that ever occurred. It is inconceivable, then, that any sequence could have occurred in any way other than that in which it did without losing its identity. Since no event could possibly have happened otherwise and still have been itself, there is not much point in singling it out and saying that it was determined. It was a consequent — but only once!

We are left with one important kind of determinism, the control of a superordinate construct over its elements. It should now become clear what is not determined. For one thing, an element does not determine the constructs which are used to subsume it; for another, an element which falls outside the purview of a construct is independent of it. The latter type of independence or freedom is relatively unimportant to us; it is only the freedom of chaos. The former type of independence or freedom is highly significant, for it implies that man, to the extent that he is able to construe his circumstances, can find for himself freedom from their domination. It implies also that man can enslave himself with his own ideas and then win his freedom again by reconstruing his life. This is, in a measure, the theme upon which this book is based.

One thing more: since determinism characterizes the control that a construct exercises over its subordinate elements, freedom characterizes its independence of those elements. Determinism and freedom are then inseparable, for that which determines another is, by the same token, free of the other. Determinism and freedom are opposite sides of the same coin — two aspects of the same relationship. This is an important point for a man to grasp, whether he be a scholar or a neurotic — or both!

Ultimately a man sets the measure of his own freedom and his own bondage by the level at which he chooses to establish his convictions. The man who orders his life in terms of many special and inflexible convictions about temporary matters makes himself the victim of circumstances. Each little prior conviction that is not open to review is a hostage he gives to fortune; it determines whether the events of tomorrow will bring happiness or misery. The man whose prior convictions encompass a broad perspective, and are cast in terms of principles rather than rules, has a much better chance of discovering those alternatives which will lead eventually to his emancipation.

Theories are the thinking of men who seek freedom amid swirling events. The theories comprise prior assumptions about certain realms of these events. To the extent that the events may, from these prior assumptions, be construed, predicted, and their relative courses charted, men may exercise control, and gain freedom for themselves in the process.

C. Design Specifications for a Psychological Theory of Personality

12. THEORETICAL MODELS AND FOCI OF CONVENIENCE

American psychology has recently turned much of its attention to the problems of theory building. There has been a revival of interest in philosophy, particularly in the philosophy of science. Just as philosophers have begun to look around to see what various kinds of thinking men are actually doing, so psychologists have begun to look around to see what kinds of theories scientists in other realms have actually been producing. This is new. To be sure, psychologists used to look to the methodology and the content of physiology as grounds upon which to build their own new structure. Then physiology was accepted because its facts were presumed to be real and its methods appeared to be validated by the palpability of its facts. But now psychologists have begun to compare and contrast the theoretical structures which characterize a variety of other disciplines. From this examination of what is going on elsewhere some of them hope to discover a still better theoretical model for psychology.

But we are skeptical about the value of copying ready-made

theories which were designed for other foci of convenience. Psychology has already achieved some success in developing its own theoretical and methodological approaches. It might now be a good plan to start abstracting the scientific principles which are beginning to emerge from our experiences as well as others', instead of poking about in the neighbors' back yards for methodological windfalls. If we learn something of the principles of theory construction, we can start building psychological theories which are adapted to psychological foci of convenience. Our position, then, would be that we should examine a variety of scientific theories, not to find one which can be copied concretely, but to discover common principles which can be applied to the building of brand-new theories especially designed to fit psychology's realm of events.

At this point there should be no doubt about our stand on two things that it takes to build a psychological theory. The perspective should be broad and should take cognizance of principles which emerge in the comparison of various theoretical structures. And the theorist should also have something to theorize about. Otherwise, he may spend his time building a fancy theory about nothing: his theory will have no focus of convenience. He should be intimately aware of a range of problems to be solved if he is not to waste his own time and that of his readers with the exposition of his theory.

The focus of convenience which we have chosen for our own theory-building efforts is the psychological reconstruction of life. We are concerned with finding better ways to help a person reconstrue his life so that he need not be the victim of his past. If the theory we construct works well within this limited range of convenience, we shall consider our efforts successful, and we shall not be too much disturbed if it proves to be less useful elsewhere.

13. FERTILITY IN A PSYCHOLOGICAL THEORY

We have already noted that a theory may be considered as a way of binding together a multitude of facts. But a good theory also performs more active functions. It provides an explicit framework within which certain deductions may be made and future events anticipated. It also provides a general framework within which certain facts may be held in place, pending one's induction of some specific principle among them. In both senses the theory acts as a tool for the man who actively seeks to anticipate the future and to explore its possibilities.

One of the criteria of a good scientific theory is its fertility in producing new ideas. It should lead to the formulation of hypotheses; it should provoke experiments; and it should inspire invention. In the field of psychology a good theory should suggest predictions concerning people's behavior in a wide range of circumstances. It should lead to extensive psychological research to determine whether or not those predictions can be substantiated. It should also encourage the invention of new approaches to the solution of the problems of man and his society.

14. TESTABLE HYPOTHESES

Another criterion of a good psychological theory is its production of hypotheses which are testable. In contrast to other construction systems, any scientific theory should enable one to make predictions so precise that they are immediately subject to incontrovertible verification. This means that the hypotheses which are deduced from the theory should be brittle enough to be shattered whenever the facts they lead one to anticipate fail to materialize.

The theory itself need not be so fragile as its offspring hypotheses. If it is a comprehensive theory it is likely to possess some degree of elasticity even though the hypotheses deduced from it are brittle. Rarely does a scientific theory wholly stand or fall on the outcome of a single crucial experiment. Especially is this true in the field of psychology, where theories must necessarily be written at a high level of abstraction.

15. VALIDITY

An acceptable scientific theory should also meet another requirement. While it need not itself have the palpable truthfulness of a cold fact, it should, in the hands of thoughtful people, yield a succession of hypotheses which, in the light of experimentation, do turn out to be palpably true. When a theory produces a hypothesis which turns out to be verifiable, it is in a strict sense the hypothesis only which is substantiated and not the theory. As we have already indicated, it is difficult ever to say that one has validated a theory; the most that one can ordinarily say is that the hypotheses turned out by a certain theory usually prove to be valid. But who knows; the same hypotheses might have been produced by other theories. In that case the other theories are at least as valid as the first one.

Sometimes scientists design experiments so that hypotheses derived from different theories are tested in competition with each other. The hypothesis which received the more clear-cut support scores in favor of its sponsoring theory. Suppose, for example, a researcher is eager to determine whether the psychoanalytic theory of Freud, with its attendant therapeutic procedures, is better than the self-concept theory of Rogers, with its attendant client-centered procedures. Suppose he sets up an elaborate experiment, controlling such tricky variables as type of client, type of therapist, type of clinical setting, type of society, and so on. Suppose, also, he finds a suitable yardstick for measuring results — one which is not biased toward either theory and its implied standards of what constitutes mental health. Then suppose — what is, of course, highly unlikely — the experiment comes off without a hitch and the results indicate a greater therapeutic success with one of the procedures than with the other. While this provides some important evidence in favor of the favored theory, it does not necessarily provide grounds for abandonment of the less favored theory. There are always other issues which can be formulated and considered. The populations sampled in the study may not represent all the kinds of persons to whom the theories relate. The relative economy of training a group of therapists under the aegis of one theory may give it certain practical advantages which outweigh its disadvantages in the controlled experiment. Indeed it is almost impossible to give any comprehensive theory the final coup de grâce.

Occasionally an experiment is designed in which the rival hypotheses are mutually incompatible. For example, one theory might lead us to hypothesize that a certain kind of client would commit suicide immediately and the other to predict that he would continue to live a long and productive life. Obviously he cannot do both. In this kind of experiment one of the two hypotheses is likely to collapse, although there is always some little ground left for equivocation. But what happens to the theory behind the discredited hypothesis? Not necessarily very much. As we have already indicated, a comprehensive theory is so formulated that the fragile hypotheses which are deduced from it are not inescapable. The deduction of a hypothesis is always a somewhat loose affair, and the next experimenter who comes along may not agree that the discredited hypothesis was a necessary derivative of the theory in the first place.

By and large, however, a theory continually yielding hypotheses that lead experimenters up blind alleys is not to be considered valid, even though one may argue that some of the blame rests with the experimenters. A theory is an implement in man's quest for a better understanding of the future. If it does not serve its purpose, it is meaningless to say that it is valid. The theory becomes valid only when someone is able to make use of it to produce verifiable hypotheses.

16. GENERALITY

Sometimes people make the mistake of assuming that a theory is the same as the accumulation of a certain body of facts, rather than a set of principles which appertain to the facts. It is easy to make this mistake, since often the facts assume their particular shapes only in the light of a certain theory. But the essentially abstract nature of the theoretical structure is lost sight of when the facts which it yields are simply classified and concretistically designated.

For example, the Kraepelinian nosological system in psychiatry is generally used as a set of diagnostic pigeonholes into which to stuff troublesome clients. The principles which originally gave it its dimensional structure have long since been discarded or lost sight of altogether. Almost without exception the system is used concretistically. Now contrast with current usage of the Kraepelinian system the use of the psychoanalytic system. Here the diagnosis is in terms of features of the case rather than its categorical classification. The diagnostician can see the case from more than one angle at once. Hence he is not so likely to confuse the abstraction of dynamics, with which each case is shot through, with the concrete lumping of the case with others of its kind.

Yet even psychoanalytic psychodynamics are often handled concretistically by adherents to the system. A patient is seen as "having Oedipal strivings," as if the strivings had taken possession of him. If the concept of Oedipal striving were used more abstractly, the patient would be evaluated with respect to the Oedipal striving dimension rather than described as "having it." The difference may seem obscure, but perhaps an analogy from physics will help make the point clearer. Suppose the physicist lifted an object and said, "By golly, this has weight!" That would not be a very meaningful statement since, presumably, all bodies have weight. Actually, he is treating the abstract property of weight as if it were a commodity. A careful physicist is much more likely to say, "The weight of this body is greater than the weight of that one." The property of weight is abstracted and the other features of the two bodies are disregarded for the time being. It is a system composed of this kind of abstraction that modern psychological theory builders seek to devise.

A good psychological theory should be expressed in terms of abstractions which are of a sufficiently high order to be traced through nearly all of the phenomena with which psychology must deal. It should concern itself initially with properties rather than with categories, although the properties may subsequently be used as grounds for isolating categories. If the abstractions are well taken, they will possess a generality which will make them useful in dealing with a great variety of practical problems. For example, if there should be abstracted within the field of psychology a property which had the generality that *mass* has in the field of physics, it might prove immensely useful. Moreover, any psychological theory that possesses generality throughout its structure is likely to be more valuable than one which is essentially a grouping of specific categories of persons and behaviors.

17. OPERATIONALISM

The writing of the physicist Bridgeman has recently had considerable influence among psychological theorists. There has been a new emphasis upon the need for operational definition of the variables envisioned in one's experiments. Carried to the extreme that some psychologists would carry it, this would mean that no theoretical statement could be made unless each part referred to something palpable. It is this kind of extremism which has led to the quip that while psychiatrists would rather be abstruse than right, psychologists would rather be wrong than abstruse.

Operationalism also implies something else. It implies that scientific constructs are best defined in terms of operations or regular sequences of events. Thus, whatever it is that links an antecedent to its consequent may be called an intervening variable, and merely a statement of the antecedent-consequent linkage is all the definition the variable ever needs. MacCorquodale and Meehl suggest that it is better for psychologists to stick to this way of conceptualizing variables lest they forget themselves and think they have to start looking for some unknown objects which constitute the variables. For example, a not too bright physiologically minded psychologist might go looking for the I.Q. with a microscope. Not that he wouldn't be successful; he might even win the Nobel Prize by pointing to something like a kink in a chromosome.

Variables may be operationally conceptualized by psychologists in different ways. In a time-and-motion study a variable may be a therblig — a unit of motion of some part of the body. The antecedent and consequent conditions are relatively easy to identify. But in some experiments the operational definition of the principal variable is more complex. In personnel selection and training studies the identification of the criterion — the measure of what it is we want to improve through selection and training — is itself a difficult problem. Yet the criterion has to be settled upon before one can get down to brass tacks. Even after the experimenters have agreed on what they will use as a criterion, the value of the ensuing study is limited by the way in which the definition has to be written. For example, in studies dealing with the selection and training of aircraft pilots it has been customary to use the so-called *pass-fail criterion* — the consequent condition is whether or not the selectee or trainee eventually gets his wings. But it is quite appropriate for a critic to complain that getting one's wings does not necessarily mean being a good pilot.

Sometimes the antecedent and consequent conditions, which are agreed upon as giving a variable an operational definition, are themselves in need of operational definition. In the field of personality the term *anxiety* is used to explain all kinds of different behaviors. Indeed, asking a psychiatrist to explain neurotic behavior without recourse to the concept of *anxiety* is like asking a jockey to win a race without riding a horse. Yet how can *anxiety* be given an operational definition? We may say that the antecedent and consequent conditions are stress and disorganization, respectively. But then we are faced with the need for defining *stress* and *disorganization*. If, eventually, we end up by saying that stress is what causes anxiety, and disorganization is what is produced by anxiety, we are back at our starting point and slightly out of breath from having expended a few thousand well-chosen words. Since *stress* and *disorganization* are both rather high-level abstractions, it is necessary, in dealing with any client or in performing any experiment involving anxiety, to find, in turn, more concrete operational definitions for the antecedent and consequent conditions.

As we see it, operationalism interposes no ultimate objection to the use of such a term as *anxiety;* it means only that when one seeks ultimate proof of some anxiety function through experimentation he will have to define his operations explicitly. Operationalism is of primary concern for the experimenter; it is of only secondary concern for the theorist. The terms in which a theory is stated do not need to carry their own operational definitions on their backs, though if the theory is to be productive it should, in the hands of experimentally minded psychologists, lead to research with operationally defined variables.

One of the hazards of operationalism is its tendency to make researchers think concretistically. It encourages experimenters to see things rather than principles. Yet, it is not things that a scientist accumulates and catalogues; it is the principles or the abstractions that strike through the things with which he is concerned. Thus a good scientist can penetrate a bewildering mass of concrete events and come to grips with an orderly principle. The principle is not the aggregate of all the events; it is rather a property, so abstracted that it can be seen as pertinent to all of them.

For example, in designing an experiment having to do with intelligence, a psychologist may have to give *intelligence* an operational definition in terms of specific scores obtained by his subjects on a certain test. This is a practical expedient. Yet, if he gets his nose too close to his data sheets, he may forget the abstractive nature of the concept and think that *intelligence* is just another name for the scores he has written down. Originally intelligence was abstracted as a property of many different behavior situations and it owes no special allegiance to a test. It was the headlong urgency of writing an operational definition that distracted the psychologist into thinking so concretively about intelligence.

18. MODIFIABILITY

There is another feature of good scientific theorizing which is not so much a property of theories themselves as it is of those who use them. A theory should be considered as modifiable and, ultimately, expendable. Sometimes theorists get so pinned down to deductive reasoning that they think their whole structure will fall down if they turn around and start modifying their assumptions in the light of their subsequent observations. One of the characteristics of modern scientific theorizing is the opening it leaves for inductive reasoning following the outcome of experiments.

To be sure, experiments are designed around hypotheses which are temporarily assumed to be true. From these tentative hypotheses one hazards specific predictions. If the predictions do not materialize, and if the scientist sees no other angle, he is free to abandon his hypotheses, and he should lose no sleep when he does. How long one should hang on to his assumptions in the face of mounting contrary evidence is pretty much a matter of taste. Certainly he should not abandon them the first time something turns out unexpectedly. To do that is to make himself the victim of circumstances. Generally one holds on longer to those assumptions which have more sweeping significance and readily abandons those which have only momentary relevance.

If we apply this principle to perseverance in a theoretical position, it would mean that we would consider any scientific theory as an eventual candidate for the trash can. Such an outlook may save the scientist a lot of anxiety, provided he has flexible overriding convictions that give him a feeling of personal independence of his theory. It may also prevent him from biasing his experimental results in favor of a theory which he dares not abandon.

19. WHAT CAN BE PROVED

The function of a scientific theory is to provide a basis for making precise predictions. These predictions are formulated in terms of hypotheses and are then subjected to test. The outcome of the test may be essentially that which was predicted. If the test or experiment is properly designed, one may then conclude, with a limited amount of confidence, that the hypothesis is substantiated.

The substantiation of hypotheses is really not quite as simple as this. The catch is in the design of the experiment. If the experiment is so designed that other obvious hypotheses would have expressed the same prediction, the question arises as to which hypothesis was verified. As a matter of fact, in scientific research, one never finds the ultimate proof of a given hypothesis. About the time he thinks he has such proof within his grasp, another scientist comes along with another hypothesis that provides just as plausible an explanation of the experimental results.

The usual practice is to design the experiment so that the results, whatever they may turn out to be, can best be expressed as the outcome of either of two hypotheses: the *experimental hypothesis* or the *null hypothesis*. The experimental hypothesis is the one derived from one's theoretical position or from some other systematic source. The null hypothesis represents one's prediction under random or chance conditions. If the data furnished by the experiment turn out to be rather unlikely outcomes of chance conditions, which is what one usually hopes for, one can turn to the experimental hypothesis as the most likely alternative explanation. For example, if the data are such as would be expected less than one time out of a hundred under the regime of chance, the experimenter reports that he has evidence at the coveted 1 per cent level of confidence. This is all very well until some imaginative experimenter cooks up a third hypothesis under which the same predictions would have been made.

The relevant point for the purposes of this discussion is that even the precise hypotheses which one derives from a good scientific theory are never substantiated with absolute finality, no matter how many experiments are performed. For one thing, we are always dependent upon the second-hand proof that the unlikelihood of the null hypothesis provides; for another, the null hypothesis never wholly relinquishes its claim on the data; and finally, some other plausible hypothesis may turn up unexpectedly at any time.

20. WHERE DO HYPOTHESES COME FROM?

There are roughly three ways of coming up with a testable hypothesis: (1) one may deduce it from explicit theory; (2) one may induce it from observation — for example, from clinical experience; (3) one may eschew logical procedures and go after it with a statistical dragnet.

Each of these methods circumvents some of the disadvantages

of the other two. The hypothetico-deductive method proceeds from a theory which, for the time being, must be considered inflexible. Sooner or later, however, the impact of unexpected experimental results must affect the logical structure, either at the hypothetical level or at the level of the theory itself. In scientific practice the question becomes one of deciding upon the stage in an experiment or in an experimental program at which one must bow to facts. That stage, wherever it is, marks the point at which one ceases to be wholly deductive.

The hypothetico-inductive method yields to facts from the outset. Even hypotheses are formulated as minor generalizations of observed facts, and the explicit theoretical superstructure is allowed to take shape more or less as an afterthought. Again, in practice, it seems to be impossible to adhere faithfully to the hypothetico-inductive method. Facts can be seen only through the eyes of observers and are subject to whatever selections and distortions the observers' viewpoints impose upon them. Realistically, then, the hypotheses formulated are personally construed facts. They may be thought of as being deduced from the observer's implicit personal theory as much as from phenomenal events.

The statistical-dragnet method also appears to accept the priority of facts. It differs from the hypothetico-inductive or clinical method in two principal ways: the logical structure, both of hypotheses and theory, is minimized; and the facts that are brought into focus have been made available by a variety of prior observations with a variety of biases.

Dragnet hypotheses are usually stated in a much less general form and, even though supported by a cross-validation procedure, cannot be extended to other situations unless certain precarious assumptions regarding the representativeness of the known samples are made. The hypotheses are usually no more than single items on a test which are predicted to be discriminative between two subsamples separated solely on the basis of a "criterion."

A dragnet picks up whatever is lying around loose. The statistical method of formulating hypotheses does just that. Variables which do not account for a sizable proportion of the measured variance in the sample are not picked up by the method, even though they may be extremely significant in bringing about personal readjustments or social changes. The hypotheses which are dredged up reflect the massed bias in the status quo.

In psychology all three methods of formulating hypotheses are employed. The hypothetico-deductive method is represented in the work of the followers of Hull's learning theory. The clinico-inductive method is represented in the work of the more scientifically minded psychoanalysts. The statistical-dragnet method is represented in the bulk of current personnel-selection test research and in the work of the Minnesota group with such tests as the Strong Vocational Interest Blank and the Minnesota Multiphasic Inventory. As long as good scientific methodology is used in checking the hypotheses, all three methods are acceptable. In using them, however, one should be aware of the bias of literalism of the hypothetico-deductive method, the personal bias in the clinico-inductive method, and the popular bias in the statistical-dragnet method.

Progress under the hypothetico-deductive method is likely to be restricted to a narrow realm for some time because of the method's inherent rigidity. The clinico-inductive method, because it aligns itself with the personal construct system of the investigator from the outset, is likely to give the impression of very rapid progress, to lead to sweeping conclusions and to cults of like-minded clinicians who establish apostolic successions for themselves through a "laying on of hands." The statistical-dragnet method provides a quick and sure exploitation of ideas that have already been expressed or applied. It tends to be sterile from the standpoint of developing new ideas, and it commonly falls into the error of assuming that the greatest volume defines the greatest truth.

21. MENTAL ENERGY IN THEORY DESIGN

Once the fundamental postulate of a theory is laid down, the variables, dimensions, and constructs with which one must be concerned start to become fixed. Also the knotty problems which sooner or later trick the scientist into intellectual contortions or into torturing his data with fancy statistical computations are likely to be traceable to the theory's fundamental postulate. It is therefore important that the fundamental postulate be chosen with the greatest of care.

In developing an alternative theoretical approach in the field of psychology it seems desirable to this writer to formulate a fundamental postulate which will obviate three of the particularly knotty problems which tend to entangle psychologists who use current theoretical approaches. The first and most important of these is the problem of explaining the impetus of psychological changes or the genesis of psychological processes. Here, most of us have unknowingly fallen heir to the physicists' ancient and implicit assumption of inert objects, objects which had to be conceived as being or as being ready to be pushed about by something. Not wishing to be animistic, the physicist called the something "energy." The scheme worked — for the physicist.

This construct of "energy" has caused particular difficulty when imported from physics into the realm of psychology. Originally introduced to explain physical change, it has been a vital feature in a variety of other scientific theories. But in the realm of psychological phenomena it has caused confusion from the outset. It has never been possible to make a very literal translation of the concept of physical "energy." It is difficult to conceive of mental "energy" as operating in anything like the closed system of economy which has been one of the useful features of its physical counterpart. In its practical application to the realm of psychology mental "energy" bears an uncomfortable resemblance to animism or even demonology.

The construct of "energy" is really an outgrowth of certain fundamental assumptions that physicists have found it convenient to make. By assuming that matter is composed basically of static units it became immediately necessary to account for the obvious fact that what was observed was not always static but often thoroughly active. What made the units active? Why "energy," of course! Psychologists, therefore, by buying the notion of "energy," had implicitly bought the same assumption of static units which had first made "energy" a necessary construct for the physicists.

For a time psychologists had trouble deciding what it was that was propelled by "energy." Was it ideas or people? At last, most psychologists agreed that it was people. But what were the vehicles for the energy which prodded these obviously inert objects into action? On the verbal level it was a simple matter to ascribe energetic properties to the elements of one's personal environment by calling them "stimuli." Or, if one preferred, he could ascribe energetic properties to aspects of the person himself; these were called "needs." Thus psychology developed *push* theories based on "stimuli" and *pull* theories based on "needs." But both approaches tended to be animistic, in that it was the "stimuli" or the "needs," rather than the person, which accounted for all the work that was done.

After berating themselves for their naïveté over a period of years, push psychologists now aver that the objects in one's environment do not really provide the energy for human acts: the notion is obviously preposterous. Instead, environmental goings-on have "stimulus functions." This means that "stimuli" are not imbued with energy — not really — it just happens to work out that way! The pull psychologists, on the other hand, insist that the "needs" and "motives" which they talk about are really no more than abstractions of human behavior. Yet these are treated as internal irritants in a creature who would otherwise continue in quiescent repose. Both theoretical groups, in their efforts to avoid an animistic interpretation of man, fall to using animistic conceptualizations of his "stimuli" and of his "needs."

Lest this appear to be a captious criticism, let it be said that any theory, scientific or opportunistic, may be considered as built upon postulates and constructs which are treated as if they were true. The acceptance of the prior assumption permits tentative formulations of conclusions and opens the way for scientific experimentation. The notions of "stimulus energy" and "need energy" do not work out too badly in this setting: they have led to many verifiable hypotheses. In this light even outright animism, in spite of its bad repute, has at times shown its worth.

There have been attempts to give a more mechanistic slant to the notions of push and pull psychology. Yet the prior assumption of the inertness of psychological objects probably makes some form of animism almost inevitable. It seems time to reconsider this prior assumption and give life back to the person who lives it.

The purpose of this discussion is to lay the groundwork for the consideration of a fundamental postulate which would obviate the necessity for a construct of mental energy. Such a postulate may make it possible to circumvent many of the knotty problems that have entangled psychologists with the constructs of "stimulus" and "stimulus function," special "needs" and "motives." One of the possibly distressing outcomes of this venture will be the discarding of much of what has been accumulated under the aegis of learning theory, perhaps even the abandonment of the concept of "learning," at least in its present form.

Instead of buying the prior assumption of an inert object, either on an implicit or explicit basis, we propose to postulate a process as the point of departure for the formulation of a psychological theory. Thus the whole controversy as to what prods an inert organism into action becomes a dead issue. Instead, the organism is delivered fresh into the psychological world alive and struggling.

Such a notion of the object of psychologists' curiosity may eventually produce an analogue for physicists to conjure with in their own domain. Indeed, some already have. The construct of matter as motion-form has already been explored by some physicists, though the yield of new testable hypotheses has not yet made the venture clearly profitable.

22. WHICH WAY WILL A MAN TURN?

Next to the problem of what accounts for the fact that a man moves at all is the problem of the direction his movement will take. This is the second of the knotty problems which tend to entangle psychologists who use current theoretical approaches. Generally psychologists have approached it with the same set of constructs which they have used to explain the fact that he moves at all. The push psychologists have assumed that each stimulus, or some resultant vector of all past stimuli put together, accounts for the direction the person takes when he is prodded into action. Similarly the pull psychologists have assumed that each need and motive carries its own special directional tendency. Thus each group derives its notions of directionality from its particular corollary to the inert-object postulate.

Field theory or Gestalt theory in psychology is an exception. Here there are certain principles which are used to account for the direction in which a man will turn, and these are more or less distinct from those which account for his merely being active. The directionality of a man's behavior is described at a higher level of abstraction than in other current theories, and some provision is made for the way the man himself structures his field.

Psychoanalysis takes no consistent theoretical stand with respect to this issue. It is perhaps best described as a theory of compromises: the compromise between the reality principle and the pleasure principle, between Todestreib and the Eros instinct, between repression and anxiety, between filial and connubial love, between action and reaction formation. Perhaps we see a Hegelian influence toward building a theory out of thesis and antithesis; perhaps we see an attempt in psychoanalysis to build a clinical theory so elastic that no hypothesis could ever be invalidated and no therapist ever discomfited.

In developing a fundamental postulate for a psychological theory of personality it would seem desirable to state it in such a way that there would always be some basis for inferring which way a person will turn when confronted with a choice situation. In this connection the psychological theorist faces an interesting problem. He must write a theory about people and what they produce. His own theory is a human production, and hence it too would need to be accounted for. Any psychological theory is therefore somewhat reflexive; it must also account for itself as a product of psychological processes. Thus, if the theory is to account for the way in which a man turns, it should also account for the way its author turned when he wrote it. This is what we were thinking of when, in an earlier section of this chapter, we proposed that we be consistent about what we conceived to be mankind's goals and what we conceived to be scientists' goals.

23. INDIVIDUALITY IN THEORY DESIGN

The third perplexing problem which may be obviated by the careful choice of a suitable basic postulate is that of explaining individual differences in a lawful manner. Psychology made rapid strides after it turned its attention to plotting the group dimensions along which men could be distinguished from each other. Progress, however, was ultimately limited. The psychology of individual differences turned out to be a psychology of group differences. Its actuarial predictions, while useful in personnel management for telling us how many students would fail, how many pilots would wash out, or even which ones had a greater likelihood of failing, nevertheless left us with few cues as to what more constructive ways could be devised for reducing failure rates, for improving instruction, for maintaining morale, for making psychotherapy more effective, or for increasing men's output of worthwhile ideas.

The problem requires some constructive approach to the relationship between private and public domains. If a man's private domain, within which his behavior aligns itself within its own lawful system, is ignored, it becomes necessary to explain him as an inert object wafted about in a public domain by external forces, or as a solitary datum sitting on its own continuum. If a man's existence in the public domain is ignored, our painstakingly acquired knowledge of one man will not help us understand his younger brother, and our daily psychological efforts will yield no increment to the cultural heritage. If both John Doe and Homo sapiens are to be construed within the same system of laws, we must lift the data from John Doe at a higher level of abstraction. It is presumptuous to construe John Doe's agitated behavior patently as "anxiety," just because it is agitated, and to bring it into the public domain as such. It may, in his particular case, be far more adequate to understand his personal construct of "kick" or "guts" or "lift" and construe it within the public domain as a form of "aggression" or "reality testing." Richard Roe's agitated behavior may, on the other hand, when proper account of his personal construct system is taken, be lifted into the public domain as a construct of "anxiety." By conceiving the individual person as himself operating under a construct system, the psychologist can lift his data from the individual case at higher levels of abstraction. It then becomes possible to build publicly a truly scientific theory around the psychology of personal constructs.

Recently there has been a resurgence of the *phenomenological* viewpoint in psychology. The original phenomenology of Husserl and Stumpf was largely swallowed up by Gestalt psychology or, more generally, by field theory. The neophenomenological point of view is perhaps best expressed by Snygg and Combs, whose basic postulate is: "All behavior, without exception, is completely determined by and pertinent to the phenomenal field of the behaving organism." The position emphasizes the fact, basic to the concept of psychology as an objective science, that the outlook of the individual person is itself a real phenomenon, no matter how badly he may misrepresent the rest of reality to himself. Since it is a real phenomenon, the psychologist is concerned with the formulation of laws and principles which explain it, and he should not assume that an erroneous view lacks any substance of its own. Moreover, the psychologist should not necessarily infer that what one person thinks has to be like what another would think in the same circumstances, nor can he accurately infer what one person thinks from what is publicly believed to be true.

Today's neophenomenology relates itself closely to what is called *self-concept theory* — the latter perhaps most clearly expressed by Raimy and Bugental. These writers are concerned with the self's position in the person's phenomenal field or, in other words, with the person's perspective of himself. Lecky's *self-consistency* position is closely allied. He emphasizes a person's urgent need for the maintenance of structure, particularly as regards himself. Thus he applies the Gestalt *law of pregnancy* to the self's seeking of integrity, and the *law of figure and ground* to the relatively greater emphasis upon self-consistency and the lesser emphasis upon consistency in external matters. On the practical side, it is Rogers who has demonstrated the fertility of these points of view in a psychotherapeutic situation. Yet here is a situation in which the inventions appeared before the theory became articulate. Rogers' *client-centered therapy* — or nondirective therapy, as it was originally called — was in full swing at Ohio State University when Raimy and Combs were students there, and Bugental was later a student of Raimy in the same department.

Rogers' systematic position, while mainly consistent with the group of positions which we have classified as neophenomenological, actually has not been stated in terms of a psychological theory. Perhaps he has been reluctant to attempt such an exposition. From his more recent writings his position appears to be more deeply rooted in certain philosophical convictions regarding the nature of man, and society's proper relationship to him, than in a set of psychological postulates.

Allport, aligning himself with Stern's later writings, has incorporated a neophenomenological type of viewpoint with the emphasis upon its methodological implications. Accepting Windelband's separation of the *nomothetic* and *idiographic* disciplines as a useful abstraction, but not as a concrete classification, he advocates a broadening of the approaches of psychology to include idiography. It is not altogether clear how logically Allport envisions the distinction between the nomothetic and the idiographic methodological approaches. Superficially the former appears to be the study of *mankind*, while the latter is the study of *a man*. Windelband considered any nomothetic discipline to be one which was concerned with general laws and which used the procedures of the exact sciences; an idiographic discipline was essentially descriptive — for example, history and biography. But the historian, in contrast to the chronicler, also derives general laws and principles which run through the mass of events that have happened. If he did not, he would be hopelessly bogged down in his newspaper files. The psychologist, too, when he describes a case, may be conducting an idiographic study; but if the description is to have any thread of meaning running through it, he must relate his selection of relevant facts to principles of human behavior. The principles, of course, may be derived within a realm no larger than the individual case, but they are still principles — they are abstractions of events.

It would be interesting and profitable to pursue further the implications of these important contributions and to pay proper respect to those who have pioneered where we have followed. But we have set out to propound a particular psychological position which seems to be promising and we must get on with it. If we stopped to pay our respects to all the thinking which has preceded and influenced what we have to say, we would never get it said. While we do not wish to appear to be historically unoriented, our plan is mainly to delineate a theoretical position for what it is and not for what its ancestry may be.

What this adds up to is that we believe it is possible to combine certain features of the neophenomenological approaches with more conventional methodology. We cannot, of course, crawl into another person's skin and peer out at the world through his eyes. We can, however, start by making inferences based primarily upon what we see him doing, rather than upon what we have seen other people doing. We have already emphasized the need to abstract behavior within the realm of the individual before making it a datum in any study of a group of individuals. Of course, when it comes to be viewed within the framework of many other individuals, it may have to be further abstracted before the useful properties begin to emerge. Thus we would be skeptical of the value of lifting a single muscle twitch as a datum from each of a thousand individuals in order to see what is happening psychologically. We would be more hopeful of abstracting the essential features in a sequence of muscle twitches in the same individual and then comparing the resultant construct with abstractions similarly anchored in other individuals' twitchings. This means, of course, that each study of an individual becomes a problem in concept formation for the psychologist. After he has conceptualized each of his cases, he next has the task of further abstracting the individual constructs in order to produce constructs which underlie people in general.

24. SUMMARY OF DESIGN SPECIFICATIONS

We are ready to commit ourselves to a fundamental postulate but, before we do so, let us review the broader framework within which the theory generated by the postulate must operate.

Mankind, whose progress in search of prediction and control of surrounding events stands out so clearly in the light of the centuries, comprises the men we see around us every day. The aspirations of the scientist are essentially the aspirations of all men.

The universe is real; it is happening all the time; it is integral; and it is open to piecemeal interpretation. Different men construe it in different ways. Since it owes no prior allegiance to any one man's construction system, it is always open to reconstruction. Some of the alternative ways of construing are better adapted to man's purposes than are others. Thus, man comes to understand his world through an infinite series of successive approximations. Since man is always faced with constructive alternatives, which he may explore if he wishes, he need not continue indefinitely to be the absolute victim either of his past history or of his present circumstances.

Life is characterized, not merely by its abstractability along a time line, but, more particularly, by the capacity of the living thing to represent its environment. Especially is this true of man, who builds construction systems through which to view the real world. The construction systems are also real, though they may be biased in their representation. Thus, both nature and human nature are phenomenologically existent.

The constructs which are hierarchically organized into systems are variously subject to test in terms of their usefulness in helping the person anticipate the course of events which make up the universe. The results of the testing of constructs determine the desirability of their temporary retention, their revision, or their immediate replacement. We assume that any system may, in proper time, have to be replaced. Within the structure of a system determinism and free will are directional aspects of the same system; that is, a construct is determined by that with which one judges it must always be consistent, and it is free of that which one judges must always be subordinated to it.

A good psychological theory has an appropriate focus and range of convenience. It suffers in usefulness when it has been transplanted from one realm to another — as, for example, from physiology to psychology. It should be fertile in producing new ideas, in generating hypotheses, in provoking experimentation, in encouraging inventions. The hypotheses which are deduced from it should be brittle enough to be testable, though the theory itself may be cast in more resilient terms. The more frequently its hypotheses turn out to be valid, the more valuable the theory.

A good psychological theory should be expressed in terms of abstractions which can be traced through most of the phenomena with which psychology must deal. In this connection, operationalism, when applied to theory construction, may interfere with the psychologist's recognition of the abstractive implications of his experimental results —he may become a laboratory technician rather than a scientist.

A psychological theory should be considered ultimately expendable. The psychologist should therefore maintain personal independence of his theory. Even experimental results never conclusively prove a theory to be ultimately true. Hypotheses are always related to some theoretical structures, but psychologists may produce them by induction or by dragnet procedures, as well as by deduction.

An attempt will be made to design a theory which will avoid the problems which are created by the implied assumptions of mental energy in push and pull theories of psychology. Such a theory would also provide a universal accounting for the alternative a man selects in a choice situation. It would recognize individuality by lifting each datum from the realm of the individual man at a relatively high level of abstraction.

Our next task is to formulate the assumptive structure which would undergird such a theory. The most basic assumption, upon which all subsequent statements must stand, is to be called a postulate. The elaboration of this statement into further, related assumptions is pursued by means of corollaries.

Chapter Two

Basic Theory

IN THIS chapter we lay down the Fundamental Postulate of our psychology of personal constructs. The theory is then elaborated by means of eleven corollaries.

A. Fundamental Postulate

1. FUNDAMENTAL POSTULATE: A PERSON'S PROCESSES ARE PSYCHO-LOGICALLY CHANNELIZED BY THE WAYS IN WHICH HE ANTICIPATES EVENTS.

Let us try to lay down a postulate which will meet the specifications we have outlined. In doing so we shall have to recognize certain limitations in our theory-building efforts. The postulate we formulate will not necessarily provide a statement from which everyone will make the same deductions. The system built upon the postulate will therefore not be completely logic-tight. Rather, we shall strive to make our theoretical position provocative, and hence fertile, rather than legalistic.

The initial statement, *a person's processes are psychologically channelized by the ways in which he anticipates events,* seems to meet our specifications. Before we go on to examine the explicit meanings and the ensuing implications of this rather simple declarative sentence, let us have a brief look at what we mean by a fundamental postulate in a scientific theory. A postulate is, of course, an assumption. But it is an assumption so basic in nature that it antecedes everything which is said in the logical system which it supports.

Now, a person may question the truth of a statement which is proposed as a fundamental postulate; indeed, we are always free, as scientists, to question the truth of anything. But we should bear in mind that the moment we do question the truth of a statement proposed as a postulate, that statement is no longer a postulate in our subsequent discourse. A statement, therefore, is a postulate only if we accord it that status. If we bring the statement into dispute, as well we may in some instances, we must recognize that we are then arguing from other postulates either explicitly stated or, more likely, implicitly believed. Thus, in scientific reasoning nothing antecedes the postulate, as long as it is a postulate, and the truth of a statement is never questioned as long as that statement is in use as a postulate.

What we have really said, then, is: let us suppose, for the sake of the discussion which is to follow, that a person's processes are psychologically channelized by the ways in which he anticipates events. Let it be clearly understood that we are not proposing this postulate as an ultimate statement of truth. In modern scientific thought it is always customary to accept even one's postulates as tentative or ad interim statements of truth and then to see what follows.

2. TERMS

Let us look at the words we have carefully chosen for this Fundamental Postulate.

a. *Person.* This term is used to indicate the substance with which we are primarily concerned. Our first consideration is the individual person rather than any part of the person, any group of persons, or any particular process manifested in the person's behavior.

b. *Processes.* Instead of postulating an inert substance, a step which would inevitably lead to the necessity for establishing, as a corollary, the existence of some sort of mental energy, the subject of psychology is assumed at the outset to be a process.

This is akin to saying that the organism is basically a behaving organism, a statement which has been emphasized by certain psychologists for some time now. But our emphasis, if anything, is even more strongly upon the kinetic nature of the substance with which we are dealing. For our purposes, the person is not an object which is temporarily in a moving state but is himself a form of motion.

c. *Psychologically.* Here we indicate the type of realm with which we intend to deal. Our theory lies within a limited realm, which is not necessarily overlapped by physiology on the one hand or by sociology on the other. Some of the phenomena which physiological systems seek to explain or which sociological systems seek to explain are admittedly outside our present field of interest and we feel no obligation to account for them within this particular theoretical structure.

As we have indicated before, we do not conceive the substance of psychology to be itself psychological — or physiological, or sociological, or to be preempted by any system. A person's processes are what they are; and psychology, physiology, or what have you, are simply systems concocted for trying to anticipate them. Thus, when we use the term *psychologically,* we mean that we are conceptualizing processes in a psychological manner, not that the processes are psychological rather than something else.

Psychology refers to a group of systems for explaining behavior, all of which seem to offer similar coverage. Thus, when we identify our system as psychological, we are loosely identifying it with certain other systems because it has a similar realm and range of convenience.

In theorizing, some people think that one ought to start out by defining the boundaries of the field of psychology. But we see no point in trying to stake out property claims for psychology's realm. The kinds of realms we are talking about are not preemptive at all — what belongs to one can still belong to another. The thing for one to do is simply erect his system and then set out to explore its range of convenience, whether that be large or small.

d. *Channelized.* We conceive a person's processes as operating through a network of pathways rather than as fluttering about in a vast emptiness. The network is flexible and is frequently modified, but it is structured and it both facilitates and restricts a person's range of action.

e. *Ways.* The channels are established as means to ends. They are laid down by the devices which a person invents in order to achieve a purpose. A person's processes, psychologically speaking, slip into the grooves which are cut out by the mechanisms he adopts for realizing his objectives.

f. *He.* Our emphasis is upon the way in which the individual man chooses to operate, rather than upon the way in which the operation might ideally be carried out. Each person may erect and utilize different ways, and it is the way he chooses which channelizes his processes.

g. *Anticipates.* Here is where we build into our theory its predictive and motivational features. Like the prototype of the scientist that he is, man seeks prediction. His structured network of pathways leads toward the future so that he may anticipate it. This is the function it serves. Anticipation is both the push and pull of the psychology of personal constructs.

h. *Events.* Man ultimately seeks to anticipate real events. This is where we see psychological processes as tied down to reality. Anticipation is not merely carried on for its own sake; it is carried on so that future reality may be better represented. It is the future which tantalizes man, not the past. Always he reaches out to the future through the window of the present.

We now have a statement of a fundamental postulate for which we have high hopes. Perhaps there can spring from it a theory of personality with movement as the phenomenon rather than the epiphenomenon, with the psychological processes of the layman making the same sense as those of the scientist, a dynamic psychology without the trappings of animism, a perceptual psychology without passivity, a behaviorism in which the behaving person is credited with having some sense, a learning theory in which learning is considered so universal that it appears in the postulate rather than as a special class of phenomena, a motivational theory in which man is neither pricked into action by the sharp points of stimuli nor dyed with the deep tones of hedonism, and a view of personality which permits psychotherapy to appear both lawful and plausible. Let us call this theory *the psychology of personal constructs.*

B. Construction Corollary

3. CONSTRUCTION COROLLARY: A PERSON ANTICIPATES EVENTS BY CONSTRUING THEIR REPLICATIONS.

In building the system which we call *the psychology of personal constructs* we have chosen to rely upon one basic postulate and to amplify the system by stating certain propositions which, in part, follow from the postulate and, in part, elaborate it in greater detail. These propositions are termed *corollaries,* although, logically, they involve somewhat more than what is minimally implied by the exact wording of the postulate. Our corollary introduces the notions of construing and replication.

4. TERMS

a. *Construing.* By construing we mean "placing an interpretation": a person places an interpretation upon what is construed. He erects a structure, within the framework of which the substance takes shape or assumes meaning. The substance which he construes does not produce the structure; the person does.

The structure which is erected by construing is essentially abstractive, though the person may be so limited in the abstraction that his construing may, in effect, be relatively concretistic. In this connection we shall need to say much more later about the forms of construing. For the present, however, since we are sketching the psychology of personal constructs in preliminary outline only, we shall not go into great detail.

In construing, the person notes features in a series of elements which characterize some of the elements and are particularly uncharacteristic of others. Thus he erects constructs of similarity and contrast. Both the similarity and the contrast are inherent in the same construct. A construct which implied similarity without contrast would represent just as much of a chaotic undifferentiated homogeneity as a construct which implied contrast without similarity would represent a chaotic particularized heterogeneity. The former would leave the person engulfed in a sea with no landmarks to relieve the monotony; the latter would confront him with an interminable series of kaleidoscopic changes in which nothing would ever appear familiar.

Construing is not to be confounded with verbal formulation. A person's behavior may be based upon many interlocking equivalence-difference patterns which are never communicated in symbolic speech. Many of these preverbal or nonverbal governing constructs are embraced in the realm of physiology. That is to say, they deal with elements which fall within the ranges of convenience of physiological construction systems. Thus they may have to do with such matters as digestion, glandular secretion, and so on, which do not normally fall within the ranges of convenience of psychological systems.

If a person is asked how he proposes to digest his dinner, he will be hard put to answer the question. It is likely that he will say that such matters are beyond his control. They seem to him to be beyond his control because he cannot anticipate them within the same system which he must use for communication. Yet digestion is an individually structured process, and what one anticipates has a great deal to do with the course it takes.

What we are saying is that the notion of construing has a wide range of convenience, if we choose to use it that way. It may even be used within borderland areas of the realm of physiology. To be sure, it operates somewhat less conveniently there, but the overlapping functions of psychological and physiological systems in this regard help to make it clear that psychology and physiology ought not to try to draw preemptive boundaries between themselves. We recognize that the psychological notion of construing has a wide range of convenience, which is by no means limited to those experiences which people can talk about or those which they can think about privately.

Construing also transcends disciplinary boundaries in another manner. A person develops a physiological construct system. We say it is a physiological construct system because it is designed around the same foci of convenience as other "physiological" systems. We are perfectly willing, therefore, to call it a "physiological" system. But that does not prevent us from examining the person's private system from a psychological point of view. Why, psychologically, did he find it convenient to look at matters this way rather than that? When we examine the personal thinking which takes the form of a physiological construction system, we may find it useful to appraise it from a psychological point of view. Thus, we may subsume a person's physiological construction system within our own psychological system.

The physiologist may turn around and do the same thing to the psychologist. He may, if he wishes, try to subsume a person's psychological system within his own professional physiological system. He may interpret ideas of grandeur in terms of physiological constructs of circulation, cortical topography, and so on. One person may subsume the constructs of A and B under the construct of C. Another may subsume B and C under A. In fact, this kind of upsetting of the hierarchical apple cart characterizes much of our day-to-day thinking, as we shall see later.

b. *Replications*. The substance that a person construes is itself a process — just as the living person is a process. It presents itself from the beginning as an unending and undifferentiated process. Only when man attunes his ear to recurrent themes in the monotonous flow does his universe begin to make sense to him. Like a musician, he must phrase his experience in order to make sense out of it. The phrases are distinguished events. The separation of events is what man produces for himself when he decides to chop up time into manageable lengths. Within these limited segments, which are based on recurrent themes, man begins to discover the bases for likenesses and differences.

Consider a day. Concretely, today is not yesterday, nor is tomorrow today. Time does not double back on itself. But after a succession of time man is able to detect a recurrent theme in its ever flowing process. It is possible to abstract the recurrent theme in terms of the rising and the setting of the sun. Moreover, the same theme does not recur when time is segmented in other ways. Thus, the concept of a day is erected along the incessant stream of time — a day which is, in its own way, like other days and yet clearly distinguishable from the moments and the years.

Once events have been given their beginnings and endings, and their similarities and contrasts construed, it becomes feasible to try to predict them, just as one predicts that a tomorrow will follow today. What is predicted is not that tomorrow will be a duplicate of today but that there are replicative aspects of tomorrow's event which may be safely predicted. Thus man anticipates events by construing their replications.

5. MATHEMATICAL IMPLICATIONS OF THE CONSTRUCTION COROLLARY

The statistics of probability are based upon the concept of replicated events. And, of course, they are also contrived to measure the predictability of further replications of the events. The two factors from which predictions are made are the number of replications already observed and the amount of similarity which can be abstracted among the replications. The latter factor involves some complicated logical problems — for example, representative sampling — and, in practice, it is the one which usually makes predictions go awry. Since the abstractive judgment of what it is that has been replicated is the basis for measuring the amount of similarity, we find that the concept-formation task which precedes the statistical manipulation of data is basic to any conclusions one reaches by mathematical logic.

The old arithmetic adage that "you can't add cows and horses" holds here. An event is replicative of another only if one is willing to accept the abstracted similarity of the two. Thus a person who owns one *cow* and one *horse* may say that he owns two *animals* — if he is willing to accept the *animal-like* abstraction of the two of them.

At a more complicated level one may average the results of

two test performances of the same person, provided, again, he is willing to accept the abstraction of the similarity in both of them. For example, one test may be a *performance* type of test and the other a *verbal* type of test. If one averages the results, what he gets is an expression of the underlying feature in both of them. If he uses a weighted average, what he gets is an expression which is a more concrete representation of the more heavily weighted test score.

We may think of it this way. All mathematical expressions, when applied to real events, are, at best, approximations. One can always question the appropriateness of the use of a statistical measure, such as chi-square, regardless of the context. The events to which this nonparametric statistic is applied must be assumed to be replications of each other. We can enter the cells of a chi-square table with cows and horses, but when we do so the cow-ness must be dropped from the cows, the horse-ness must be dropped from the horses, and only the animal-ness in both of them allowed to remain. Thus, whenever one uses the chi-square statistic, he must be aware of the abstractive implications in his data. What one could conclude from a chi-square computation from a table in which both cows and horses had been entered is that, *in the sense that cows and horses are replicated events, such and such is true of them.*

We have been talking about the mathematical expression of chi-square. What we have said might have been said about simple enumeration. We point to each of a series of things and count: *one, two, three. . . .* The counting makes sense if the things are distinguishable from each other, and it makes sense only in the respect that they are alike. Before we can count them we must construe their concrete difference from each other, their abstract likeness to each other, and their abstract difference from other things which are not to be counted. We must be able to construe where one thing leaves off and another begins, which one is similar enough to the others to be counted, and what is extraneous. What we count depends on what we abstract to be counted; thus, any mathematical expression relies upon the concept-formation task which has preceded it. Mathematical manipulation does not reify data, though it often provides a handy way of testing the adequacy of our conceptualizations.

What we are saying is that when a person anticipates events by construing their replications, he lays the ground for mathematical reasoning. All mathematical reasoning is utterly dependent upon the premathematical construing process which gives it something to enumerate. We think this is important.

C. Individuality Corollary

6. INDIVIDUALITY COROLLARY: PERSONS DIFFER FROM EACH OTHER IN THEIR CONSTRUCTION OF EVENTS.

Since our Fundamental Postulate throws our emphasis upon the ways in which a person anticipates events, it provides grounds for a psychology of individual differences. People can be seen as differing from each other, not only because there may have been differences in the events which they have sought to anticipate, but also because there are different approaches to the anticipation of the same events.

Persons anticipate both public events and private events. Some writers have considered it advisable to try to distinguish between "external" events and "internal" events. In our system there is no particular need for making this kind of distinction. Nor do we have to distinguish so sharply between stimulus and response, between the organism and his environment, or between the self and the not-self.

No two people can play precisely the same role in the same event, no matter how closely they are associated. For one thing, in such an event, each experiences the other as an external figure. For another, each experiences a different person as the central figure (namely, himself). Finally, the chances are that, in the course of events, each will get caught up in a different stream and hence be confronted with different navigational problems.

But does this mean that there can be no sharing of experience? Not at all; for each may construe the likenesses and differences between the events in which he himself is involved, together with those in which he sees that the other person is involved. Thus, while there are individual differences in the construction of events, persons can find common ground through construing the experiences of their neighbors along with their own. It is not inevitable that they should come upon such common ground; indeed, where the cultural identifications are different or where one person has given up seeking common ground with his neighbors, individuals can be found living out their existence next door to each other but in altogether different subjective worlds.

D. Organization Corollary

7. ORGANIZATION COROLLARY: EACH PERSON CHARACTERISTICALLY EVOLVES, FOR HIS CONVENIENCE IN ANTICIPATING EVENTS, A CONSTRUCTION SYSTEM EMBRACING ORDINAL RELATIONSHIPS BETWEEN CONSTRUCTS.

Different constructs sometimes lead to incompatible predictions, as everyone who has experienced personal conflict is painfully aware. Man, therefore, finds it necessary to develop ways of anticipating events which transcend contradictions. Not only do men differ in their constructions of events, but they also differ in the ways they organize their constructions of events. One man may resolve the conflicts between his anticipations by means of an ethical system. Another may resolve them in terms of self-preservation. The same man may resolve in one way at one time and in the other way at another. It all depends upon how he backs off to get perspective.

8. TERMS

a. *Characteristically.* Again we emphasize the personalistic nature of the process: here in the case of the system. Not only are the constructs personal, but the hierarchical system into which they are arranged is personal too. It is this systematic arrangement which characterizes the personality, even more than do the differences between individual constructs.

b. *Evolves.* The construction system does not stand still, although it is relatively more stable than the individual constructs of which it is composed. It is continually taking new shape. This is a way of saying that the personality is continually taking new shape. Deep psychotherapy may help a person with this evolvement and thus possibly accomplish important readjustments in a person's style of life.

c. *Construction system.* A system implies a grouping of elements in which incompatibilities and inconsistencies have been minimized. They do not disappear altogether, of course. The systematization helps the person to avoid making contradictory predictions.

d. *Ordinal relationships between constructs.* One construct may subsume another as one of its elements. It may do this in either of two ways; it may extend the cleavage intended by the other or it may abstract across the other's cleavage line. For example, the construct *good vs. bad* may subsume, respectively, among other things, the two ends of the intelligent-stupid dimension. In this sense, "good" would include all "intelligent" things plus some things which fall outside the range of convenience of the *intelligent vs. stupid* construct. "Bad" would include all the "stupid" things plus some others which are neither "intelligent" nor "stupid." This is what we mean by extending the cleavage intended by the construct *intelligent vs. stupid.*

An example of abstracting across the *intelligent vs. stupid* cleavage line would be the construct of *evaluative vs. descriptive.* In this case the *intelligent vs. stupid* construct would be subsumed as a dimension. The construct would itself be identified as an "evaluative" type of construct and would be contrasted with other constructs such as *light vs. dark,* which might be considered "descriptive" only. Both *good vs. bad* and *evaluative vs. descriptive* may thus be used as superordinating constructs, the former in what some writers would call an "absolutistic" sense and the latter in what they would call a "relativistic" sense.

Within a construction system there may be many levels of ordinal relationships, with some constructs subsuming others and those, in turn, subsuming still others. When one construct subsumes another its ordinal relationship may be termed *super-*

ordinal and the ordinal relationship of the other becomes *subordinal*. Moreover, the ordinal relationship between the constructs may reverse itself from time to time. For example, "intelligent" may embrace all things "good" together with all things "evaluative," and "stupid" would be the term for "bad" and "descriptive" things; or, if the other kind of subsuming is involved, "intelligent" might embrace the construct *evaluative vs. descriptive* while "stupid" would be the term for the *good vs. bad* dichotomy. Thus man systematizes his constructs by concretely arranging them in hierarchies and by abstracting them further. But whether he pyramids his ideas or penetrates them with insights, he builds a system embracing ordinal relationships between constructs for his personal convenience in anticipating events.

9. IMPLICATIONS OF THE ORGANIZATION COROLLARY

The pursuit of implications arising out of our assumptive structure is the major objective of the chapters which follow. However, it may be helpful to offer some passing hints as to the practical implications of our corollaries. The Organization Corollary is basic to our understanding of that most common of all clinic commodities, anxiety. It also sets the stage for the way we shall look upon the clinic client's mirrored image of himself.

Thus far we have said that the person is bent on anticipating events. His psychological processes are channelized with this in mind. Each person attunes his ear to the replicative themes he hears and each attunes his ear in a somewhat different way. But it is not mere certainty that man seeks; if that were so, he might take great delight in the repetitive ticking of the clock. More and more he seeks to anticipate all impending events of whatsoever nature. This means that he must develop a system in which the most unusual future can be anticipated in terms of a replicated aspect of the familiar past.

Now it so happens that a person must occasionally decide what to do about remodeling his system. He may find the job long overdue. How much can he tear down and still have a roof over his head? How disruptive will a new set of ideas be?

Dare he jeopardize the system in order to replace some of its constituent parts? Here is the point at which he must choose between preserving the integrity of the system and replacing one of its obviously faulty parts. Sometimes his anticipation of events will be more effective if he chooses to conserve the system. It is precisely at this point that the psychotherapist may fail to understand why his client is so resistive. It is also at this point that he may do his client harm.

Lecky has emphasized a person's need for self-consistency. In doing so he has thrown particular emphasis upon the preservation of those aspects of one's system which have to do with the self. Certain essential features of what Lecky says are, in effect, reiterated here, and we are indebted to him. However, our view is that it is not consistency for consistency's sake nor even self-consistency that gives man his place in the world of events. Rather, it is his seeking to anticipate the whole world of events and thus relate himself to them that best explains his psychological processes. If he acts to preserve the system, it is because the system is an essential chart for his personal adventures, not because it is a self-contained island of meaning in an ocean of inconsequentialities.

E. Dichotomy Corollary

10. DICHOTOMY COROLLARY: A PERSON'S CONSTRUCTION SYSTEM IS COMPOSED OF A FINITE NUMBER OF DICHOTOMOUS CONSTRUCTS.

We have already said that a person anticipates events by noting their replicative aspects. Having chosen an aspect with respect to which two events are replications of each other, we find that, by the same token, another event is definitely not a replication of the first two. The person's choice of an aspect determines both what shall be considered similar and what shall be considered contrasting. The same aspect, or the same abstraction, determines both. If we choose an aspect in which A and B are similar, but in contrast to C, it is important to note that it is the same aspect of all three, A, B, *and* C, that forms the basis of the construct. It is not that there is one aspect of A and B that makes them similar to each other and another aspect that makes them contrasting to C. What we mean is that there is an aspect of A, B, and C which we may call z. With respect to this aspect, A and B are similar and C stands in contrast to them. This is an important notion, for on it is built much of the technical procedure that characterizes the psychology of personal constructs.

Let us pursue our model further. Let us suppose that there is an element O in which one is unable to construe the aspect of z. O then falls outside the range of convenience of the construct based on z. The aspect of z is irrelevant in that part of the realm occupied by O. Not so C, however. The aspect of z is quite relevant to C. It is z that enables us to differentiate between C and the two similar elements, A and B. The aspect of z performs no such service in helping us discriminate between O and the two similar elements, A and B.

Suppose, for example, A and B are men, C is a woman, and O is the time of day. We abstract an aspect of A, B, and C which we may call *sex*. Sex, then, is our z. Sex is not applicable to O, the time of day; at least most of us would not so abstract it. The time of day, O, does not fall within the range of convenience of the construct of sex, z. Now, with respect to sex, z, the two men, A and B, are alike and in contrast to the woman, C. Moreover, the construct is no less applicable to the woman, C, than it is to the two men, A and B.

But suppose we say that the construct is not sex, z, but masculinity, y. Then is not the woman, C, just as unmasculine as the time of day, O? Our answer is no. She is much more relevantly unmasculine than is the time of day. The notion of masculinity is predicated upon a companion notion of femininity, and it is the two of them together which constitute the basis of the construct. Masculinity would mean nothing if it were not for femininity. There would be no point in using the term *man* in the masculine sense if it were not for the notion of sex.

What we propose to do is to assume that all constructs follow this basic dichotomous form. Inside its particular range of convenience a construct denotes an aspect of all the elements lying therein. Outside this range of convenience the aspect is not recognizable. Moreover, the aspect, once noted, is meaningful only because it forms the basis of similarity and contrast between the elements in which it is noted. In laying down this assumption we are departing from the position of classical logic. But we suspect that this comes nearer representing the way people actually think. In any case, we propose to pursue the implications of this assumption and see where we are led.

11. TERMS

a. *Composed.* By this we mean that the system is composed entirely of constructs. It consists of nothing but constructs. Its organizational structure is based upon constructs of constructs, concretistically pyramided or abstractly cross-referenced in a system of ordinal relationships.

b. *Dichotomous constructs.* The construct denotes an aspect of the elements lying within its range of convenience, on the basis of which some of the elements are similar to others and some are in contrast. In its minimum context a construct is a way in which at least two elements are similar and contrast with a third. There must therefore be at least three elements in the context. There may, of course, be many more.

c. *Finite number.* Man's thinking is not completely fluid; it is channelized. If he wants to think about something he must follow the network of channels he has laid down for himself, and only by recombining old channels can he create new ones. These channels structure his thinking and limit his access to the ideas of others. We see these channels existing in the form of constructs.

12. IMPLICATIONS OF THE DICHOTOMY COROLLARY

But do people really think in terms of dichotomies? Do they always abstract on the basis of both similarity and contrast? These are questions which are bound to be asked. Since they challenge a part of our assumptive structure, we would have to step outside our system in order to try to answer them. We can, however, clarify the assumption somewhat further and thus perhaps make it more acceptable for the time being.

Not long ago a client said, in effect, to her therapist, "I believe that everything in the world is good. There is nothing bad. All people are good. All inanimate things are good. All thoughts are good." These statements, faintly suggestive of Voltaire's *Candide,* alerted the clinician to a probable underlying hostility. Obviously the client's statement was intended to mean something; the therapist's task was to find the implied contrast which she was unable to put into words.

The client could have meant several things. She could have meant that everything is now good whereas formerly it was bad. She could have been denying the good-bad dimension as a meaningful dimension and have chosen to do so by asserting the universality of one end of the dimension. She could have meant that everything other than herself was good. Or she could have meant that she was one who saw good in everything whereas others were seers of the bad. As matters turned out, she was expressing her construct in the latter two senses. She meant, "I suspect that I am bad and I suspect that you see me as bad, even though I have the compensating virtue of myself being willing to see everyone as good." There is a suggestion of what the clinicians call "an idea of reference" here, and the way the client expressed it suggests what some clinicians call "acting out."

Perhaps this illustration will suffice, for the time being, to indicate how the Dichotomy Corollary affects the clinician in dealing with his client. Instead of seeing his client as the victim of a submerged conflict between opposing instinctual forces, he sees the dichotomy as an essential feature of thinking itself. As he seeks to understand what his client means, he looks for the elements in the construct context. As long as he approaches man's thinking from the standpoint of formal logic, it is impossible for him to comprehend any thinking which man is unable to verbalize. But as we approach man's thinking psychologically, using both the clinical and the more fragmentary methods of investigation, we can see the operational dichotomization of his constructs into similarities and contrasts.

Much of our language, as well as of our everyday thinking,

implies contrast which it does not explicitly state. Our speech would be meaningless otherwise. If we proceed on this assumption, we may be able to gain insights into the psychological processes which have long been concealed by a formal logic which was altogether too much shackled by words.

How does our notion of dichotomous constructs apply to such "class concepts" as *red?* Is *red* a statement of contrast as well as of similarity? We might point out that, according to one of the prevalent color theories, red is the complement of green. Among the hues it stands in sharpest contrast to green. But *red* is used in other ways also. When we say that a person has red hair we are distinguishing it from the nonredness of white, yellow, brown, or black. Our language gives no special word for this nonredness, but we have little difficulty in knowing what the contrast to red hair actually is.

Similarly other constructs, such as *table,* express, within their ranges of convenience, both likenesses and differences. The differences are just as relevant as the likenesses; they are applicable within the constructs' ranges of convenience. Unlike classical logic, we do not lump together the contrasting and the irrelevant. We consider the contrasting end of a construct to be both relevant and necessary to the meaning of the construct. It falls within the range of convenience of the construct, not outside. Thus the construct of *table* has meaning, not merely because a series of objects, called *tables,* are similar to each other in this respect, but also because certain other objects of furniture stand in contrast in this same respect. For example, it makes sense to point to a chair and say, "That is not a table." It makes no sense to point to a sunset and say, "That is not a table."

The Dichotomy Corollary assumes a structure of psychological processes which lends itself to binary mathematical analysis. The concepts of modern physics, particularly electron theory, and the devices, such as the vacuum tube, which have been developed as the implements of those concepts, are having a far-reaching influence these days. The practical task of reducing information to a form which can be handled by electronic computing machines has forced scientists to reconsider the mathematical structure of knowledge itself. Psychology, for a half century an initiator of mathematical inventions relating to human behavior, is now itself caught up in the new nonparametric mathematics. Personal-construct theory, with its emphasis upon the dichotomous nature of the personal constructs which channelize psychological processes, is in full accord with this modern trend in scientific thinking. But personal-construct theory would not lose sight of premathematical construct formation. A sorting machine, no matter how complex, is not a thinking machine as long as we have to select data to feed into it.

F. Choice Corollary

13. CHOICE COROLLARY: A PERSON CHOOSES FOR HIMSELF THAT ALTERNATIVE IN A DICHOTOMIZED CONSTRUCT THROUGH WHICH HE ANTICIPATES THE GREATER POSSIBILITY FOR EXTENSION AND DEFINITION OF HIS SYSTEM.

If a person's processes are psychologically channelized by the ways in which he anticipates events, and those ways present themselves in dichotomous form, it follows that he must choose between the poles of his dichotomies in a manner which is predicted by his anticipations. We assume, therefore, that whenever a person is confronted with the opportunity for making a choice, he will tend to make that choice in favor of the alternative which seems to provide the best basis for anticipating the ensuing events.

Here is where inner turmoil so frequently manifests itself. Which shall a man choose, security or adventure? Shall he choose that which leads to immediate certainty or shall he choose that which may eventually give him a wider understanding? For the man of constricted outlook whose world begins to crumble, death may appear to provide the only immediate certainty which he can lay hands on. And yet, in the words of Shakespeare's Hamlet,

> But that the dread of something after death —
> The undiscover'd country, from whose bourn

No traveler returns — puzzles the will;
And makes us rather bear those ills we have
Than fly to others that we know not of?

Whatever the breadth of his viewpoint, it is our assumption that man makes his choice in such a fashion as to enhance his anticipations. If he constricts his field of vision, he can turn his attention toward the clear definition of his system of constructs. If he is willing to tolerate some day-by-day uncertainties, he may broaden his field of vision and thus hope to extend the predictive range of the system. Whichever his choice may be — for constricted certainty or for broadened understanding — his decision is essentially elaborative. He makes what we shall call hereinafter *the elaborative choice*.

14. TERMS

a. *Chooses*. Not only is a person's construction system composed of dichotomous constructs but, within the system of dichotomies, the person builds his life upon one or the other of the alternatives represented in each of the dichotomies. This is to say that he places relative values upon the ends of his dichotomies. Some of the values are quite transient and represent merely the convenience of the moment. Others are quite stable and represent guiding principles. Even the stable ones are not necessarily highly intellectualized — they may appear, rather, as appetitive preferences.

b. *For himself*. When one makes a choice he involves himself in the selection. Even if the choice is no more than a temporary hypothesis explored in the course of solving a mathematical problem or in looking for a lost screwdriver, he must perceive himself as being modified through the chain of ensuing events. Some of his choices will seem to be major turning points in his life; others may appear to be no more than a passing impulse — a decision to glance to the left rather than to the right.

c. *Alternative*. If a person sets up the construct of *black vs. white*, an object cannot, for him, be both black and white. The construct tends to force upon him either one or the other of the two alternatives. If it were not so, the construct would have no meaning.

What about shades of gray? While the construct of *black vs. white* is composed of mutually exclusive alternatives, this does not preclude the use of the construct in a relativistic manner. Relativism is not the same as ambiguity, although some persons try to construe it that way. Of two objects, one may be blacker than the other; but it cannot be blacker than the other and at the same time the other be blacker than it is. As we shall see later, dichotomous constructs can be built into scales, the scales representing superordinate constructs which are further abstractions of the separate scalar values. Thus, *more grayness vs. less grayness* is a further abstraction of the construct *black vs. white*.

d. *Through.* We must keep in mind that constructs have to do with processes and not merely with the spatial arrangement of static objects. The use of the constructs is itself a process also. Thus the use of constructs is a matter of choosing vestibules *through* which one passes during the course of his day.

e. *Anticipates.* Since we have postulated that all human movement is based on anticipations, the choice of an alternative through which to move is itself a matter of what one anticipates.

f. *Greater possibility.* Not only is one's choice based upon the anticipation of some particular thing, but it may also be based upon one's anticipation of things in general. A person does not have to know specifically what it is that he expects in order to make his elaborative choice. He can go fishing, choosing only a well-stocked stream.

g. *Extension.* Instead of saying that one makes his choice in favor of the alternative that seems to offer the greater possibility for extension and definition, we might have said that he makes his choice in favor of the greater possibility for further elaboration of the system. But we wish to make it clear that elaboration of one's construct system can be in the direction either of extension or of definition, or of both. The extension of the system includes making it more comprehensive, increasing its range of convenience, making more and more of life's experiences meaningful.

h. *Definition.* The principle of the elaborative choice also includes a person's tendency to move toward that which appears to make his system more explicit and clear cut. As we have already indicated, this may, in some instances, appear to call for constriction of one's field — even to the point of ultimate constriction, suicide. Internal conflict, as in the case of Hamlet, is often a matter of trying to balance off the secure definiteness of a narrowly encompassed world against the uncertain possibilities of life's adventure. One may anticipate events by trying to become more and more certain about fewer and fewer things or by trying to become vaguely aware of more and more things on the misty horizon.

i. *His system.* Here we emphasize the assumption that, while it is events that one seeks to anticipate, he makes his elaborative choice in order to define or extend the system which he has found useful in anticipating those events. We might call this "a seeking of self-protection," or "acting in defense of the self," or "the preservation of one's integrity." But it seems more meaningful to keep clearly in mind what the self is, what it is designed to do, and what integral function is served. Thus we hope it is clear that what we assume is that the person makes his choice in favor of elaborating a system which is functionally integral with respect to the anticipation of events. To us it seems meaningless to mention a system qua system. It must be a system *for something.* From our point of view a person's construction system is for the anticipation of events. If it were for something else, it would probably shape up into something quite different.

15. IMPLICATIONS OF THE CHOICE COROLLARY

The Choice Corollary lays down the grounds upon which we can make some predictions regarding how people will act after they have construed the issues with which they are faced. Frequently the therapist finds it difficult to understand why his client, in spite of insights which would appear to make it clear how he should behave, continues to make the "wrong" choices. The therapist, seeing only the single issue which he has helped the client to define, often fails to realize that, within the system of personal constructs which the client has erected, the decision for action is not necessarily based on that issue alone but on a complex of issues.

For example, no matter how obvious it may be that a person would be better off if he avoided a fight or spoke pleasantly to his boss, it may so happen that such a course of action would seem to him personally to limit the definition and extension of his system as a whole. He may, therefore, in spite of the neatest psychotherapeutic interpretations, continue to quarrel with his neighbors and to snub anyone who seems to be invested with authority. The Choice Corollary, therefore, suggests ways in which a therapeutic program can go beyond mere intellectual insight and how it might enable the client to enter the experimental phases of the program.

Under the Choice Corollary we are able to reconstrue some of the issues for which hedonism and motivational theory provide awkward answers. Stimulus-response theory requires some sorts of assumptions to explain why certain responses become linked to certain stimuli. In certain theoretical structures this is managed by some supplementary theorizing about the nature of motives or need satisfactions. But in our assumptive structure we do not specify, nor do we imply, that a person seeks "pleasure," that he has special "needs," that there are "rewards," or even that there are "satisfactions." In this sense, ours is not a commercial theory. To our way of thinking, there is a continuing movement toward the anticipation of events, rather than a series of barters for temporal satisfactions, and this movement is the essence of human life itself.

G. Range Corollary

16. RANGE COROLLARY: A CONSTRUCT IS CONVENIENT FOR THE AN-
   TICIPATION OF A FINITE RANGE OF EVENTS ONLY.

Just as a system or a theory has its focus and range of convenience, so a personal construct has a focus and range of convenience. There are few if any personal constructs which one can say are relevant to everything. Even such a construct as *good vs. bad,* in its personalized form, is not likely to be considered by the user to be applicable throughout the range of his perceptual field. Of course, some persons use the construct more comprehensively than others; but, even so, they are inclined to erect boundaries of convenience beyond which elements are neither good nor bad. A construct of *tall vs. short* is much easier to see as having a limited range of convenience. One may construe tall houses versus short houses, tall people versus short people, tall trees versus short trees. But one does not find it convenient to construe tall weather versus short weather, tall light versus short light, or tall fear versus short fear. Weather, light, and fear are, for most of us at least, clearly outside the range of convenience of *tall vs. short.*

Sometimes one is surprised to learn how narrowly a certain person applies some of his constructs. For example, one person may use the construct of *respect vs. contempt* to apply broadly to many different kinds of interpersonal relationships. Another person may use it to apply only to a very narrow range of events, perhaps only to the choice of words in a formally structured situation, such as a court proceeding.

As we have indicated before, in our discussion of the Dichotomy Corollary, our position here is somewhat different from that of classical logic. We see relevant similarity and contrast as essential and complementary features of the same construct and both of them as existing within the range of convenience of the construct. That which is outside the range of convenience of the construct is not considered part of the contrasting field but simply an area of irrelevancy.

While we have not said so before, it is probably apparent by now that we use the term *construct* in a manner which is somewhat parallel to the common usage of "concept." However, if one attempts to translate our *construct* into the more familiar term, "concept," he may find some confusion. We have included, as indeed some recent users of the term "concept" have done, the more concretistic concepts which nineteenth-century psychologists would have insisted upon calling "percepts." The notion of a "percept" has always carried the idea of its being a personal act — in that sense, our *construct* is in the tradition of "percepts." But we also see our *construct* as involving abstraction — in that sense our *construct* bears a resemblance to the traditional usage of "concept." And finally, we prefer the use of the term *construct* because, as a term, it has emerged more within the context of experimental psychology than within the context of mentalistic psychology or of formal logic.

Now when we assume that the construct is basically dichotomous, that it includes percepts, and that it is a better term for our purposes than the term "concept," we are not quarreling with those who would use it otherwise. Within some systems of logic the notion of contrast as something distinct from irrelevancy is not part of the assumptive structure. We, on the other hand, are simply assuming that this is the way people do, in fact, think. We shall operate upon this assumption until it begins to appear that our theory is failing to measure up to the standards we outlined in the preceding chapter. We do not insist that people ought to think in this way, nor are we greatly concerned if others believe that people ought to think in the classical way. Ours is simply a psychological theory, and the nature of personal constructs is built into the assumptive structure.

17. IMPLICATIONS OF THE RANGE COROLLARY

The Range Corollary, together with the Dichotomy Corollary, provides a somewhat new approach to the analysis of human thought processes. Consider a given person's use of the construct of *respect vs. contempt*. Under conventional logic one would consider these as two separate concepts. If we wished to understand the person's use of the term "respect," we might seek to find out how broadly he applied the term — how he "generalized the concept." We would want to know what acts he considered to be characterized by "respect" and what acts he did not consider "respectful." Thus we might be able to discover by the method of varying concomitants just what abstraction among the acts he had been able to make.

But when we approach the thinking of a person, say a clinic

client, in this way, we miss a great deal. We miss it because we are tacitly assuming that everything which he does not construe as "respect" is irrelevant. Yet his use of the construct may be particularly meaningful because of what he excludes rather than because of what he includes. When we approach his thinking from the standpoint of the psychology of personal constructs, we do not lump together what he excludes as irrelevant with what he excludes as contrasting. We see the construct as composed essentially of a *similarity-contrast* dimension which he strikes through a part of his field of experience. We need to look at both ends of it if we want to know what it means to him. We cannot understand him well if we look only at the similarity — "respect" — end of the dimension. We cannot understand what he means by "respect" unless we know what he sees as relevantly opposed to "respect."

The psychologist who employs the approach of the psychology of personal constructs is led always to look for the contrasting elements of his client's constructs as well as the similar elements. Until he has some notion of the contrast, he does not presume to understand the similarity. He would therefore seek to understand what his client construed as the opposite of respect and what the range of convenience of the whole construct covered. As his client continues to talk about the construct of "respect," the psychologist may discover just what it is that the client is condemning, by implication, as contemptuous or contemptible.

Freud found that he needed to understand what his clients meant by what they *did not say*. He used the notions of "repression" and "reaction formation" to explain what he observed. These he saw as perverse tendencies, somewhat characteristic of all men but particularly of certain disturbed persons. Our position is that contrast is an essential feature of all personal constructs, a feature upon which their very meaning depends. We would agree with Freud that there are instances in which the person is so self-involved with a construct that he avoids expressing its contrasting aspect lest he misidentify himself.

In practice, then, one looks not only for the similarities but also for the contrasts in understanding a client's construct. Moreover, he looks to see how extensive is the range of convenience of the construct, both for the similar elements and for the contrast elements. Until he understands how extensively the contrast is construed, he cannot realize the full import of the client's thinking.

H. Experience Corollary

18. EXPERIENCE COROLLARY: A PERSON'S CONSTRUCTION SYSTEM VARIES AS HE SUCCESSIVELY CONSTRUES THE REPLICATIONS OF EVENTS.

Since our Fundamental Postulate establishes the anticipation of events as the objective of psychological processes, it follows that the successive revelation of events invites the person to place new constructions upon them whenever something unexpected happens. Otherwise one's anticipations would become less and less realistic. The succession of events in the course of time continually subjects a person's construction system to a validation process. The constructions one places upon events are working hypotheses, which are about to be put to the test of experience. As one's anticipations or hypotheses are successively revised in the light of the unfolding sequence of events, the construction system undergoes a progressive evolution. The person reconstrues. This is experience. The reconstruction of one's life is based upon just this kind of experience. We have tried to express this implication of our Fundamental Postulate in the Experience Corollary.

19. TERMS

a. *System.* We have already indicated that a system implies a grouping of elements in which incompatibilities and inconsistencies have been minimized. We have also indicated that a person's construction system involves ordinal relationships between constructs. Construction is systematic in that it falls into a pattern having features of regularity. Since construing is a kind of refinement process involving abstraction and generalization, it is a way of looking at events as having a kind of identity with each other and as not being wholly unique. These features of identity and regularity are given shape through construction, which itself has been shaped up as a system.

b. *Varies*. The changes in the construction system are not always "for the good" nor do they necessarily always tend to stabilize. They do vary, however. The variation may disrupt the system and lead to further and more rapid variation. It may precipitate a major shake-up in the system. Contrariwise, the variation may stabilize the system and make its basic features resistant to further modification.

c. *Successively*. Construing, like all processes, may be chopped up into segments having beginnings and endings. Construing may itself be considered a sequence of events. Segmented in this manner it is proper to speak of construing as taking place successively. Like other features of life, its principal dimension is time, and it is itself a process, a phenomenon. The events of one's construing march single file along the path of time.

d. *Replications of events*. As new events are added to the record of those which have passed, the person has an opportunity to reconsider the replicative aspects which link the recent with the remote. What is it which has been repeated? What now constitutes the recurrent theme? Concretely, the new events are unique; it is only by abstracting them that the person finds that which is replicated.

20. EXPERIENCE, ORDERLINESS, AND TIME

By calling this corollary the Experience Corollary we indicate what we assume to be the essential nature of experience. Experience is made up of the successive construing of events. It is not constituted merely by the succession of events themselves. A person can be a witness to a tremendous parade of episodes and yet, if he fails to keep making something out of them, or if he waits until they have all occurred before he attempts to reconstrue them, he gains little in the way of experience from having been around when they happened. It is not what happens around him that makes a man experienced; it is the successive construing and reconstruing of what happens, as it happens, that enriches the experience of his life.

Our corollary also throws emphasis upon construing the replicative features of experience. The person who merely stands agog at each emerging event may experience a series of interesting surprises, but if he makes no attempt to discover the recurrent themes, his experience does not amount to much. It is when man begins to see the orderliness in a sequence of events that he begins to experience them.

The notion of an organized and potentially lawful universe has not been easy for men to accept. How can one accept lawfulness unless he can state the law? Must not one resort to anthropomorphism whenever his predictions go awry? Should we not attribute all such unexpected events to "manlike" caprice? There are actually some scientists who see great orderliness within their physical frames of reference but who throw up their hands and say, "There must be a psychological factor," whenever they fail to find orderliness. This might be all right if what they meant was that it was time to apply some psychological constructs. But what they usually mean is that the phenomena are disorderly.

Sometimes the notion of the world as an orderly development of events seems downright threatening to a person. Particularly is this likely to be true when he deals with psychological events. If he sees orderliness in the behavior of a friend or in his own behavior, it seems to preclude the possibility of seeing the actions of either as being free. This is a personal problem that the psychotherapist must frequently face in trying to help his client. If the client perceives himself as an orderly succession of events, he feels trapped by his own structure or by the events of his biography. Yet, if he sees himself as deciding each moment what he shall do next, it may seem as though one little false step will destroy his integrity.

In spite of the personal hazards and the difficulties of construing the succession of events which make up his universe, man has gradually extended his constructs of orderliness through the centuries. Perhaps he first perceived orderliness in the stately procession that marched across the night sky. Perhaps he first saw replication in the rolling of a stone along the ground and, from its rapid succession of events, was able to construct the notion of cycles and epicyles. Perhaps it came much earlier, as he detected the beating of his own pulse. But wherever it started, man's widening awareness of the universe as an orderly unfolding of events gave him increased capacity to predict and made his world more and more manageable. Even rare cataclysms assumed the familiarity of *déja vu*. Man gradually discovered that he could lay a sight on the future through the experience of the past.

The essential referent dimension along which all orderliness and organization must be construed is that of time. Except as there is a seasonable replication of events or aspects of events, no organization whatsoever can be ascribed to the universe and there is no such thing as experience. The discovery of replicative themes is not only the key to experience, it is the key to natural law.

21. EXPERIENCE AND LEARNING

The Experience Corollary has profound implications for our thinking about the topic of learning. When we accept the assumption that a person's construction system varies as he successively construes the replications of events, together with the antecedent assumption that the course of all psychological processes is plotted by one's construction of events, we have pretty well bracketed the topic of learning. What has been commonly called "learning" has been covered at the very outset. Learning is assumed to take place. It has been built into the assumptive structure of the system. The question of whether or not it takes place, or what is learned and what is not learned, is no longer a topic for debate within the system we have proposed. Of course, if we wish to step outside the system and argue within the framework of some other system, we can take sides on these topics.

The burden of our assumption is that learning is not a special class of psychological processes; it is synonymous with any and all psychological processes. It is not something that happens to a person on occasion; it is what makes him a person in the first place.

The net effect of incorporating learning into the assumptive structure of a psychological theory is to remove the whole topic from the realm of subsequent discourse. Some readers may be dismayed at this turn of events. Psychology now has a considerable investment of research effort in the topic. But psychology's investment is not altogether depreciated by the new set of assumptions, even though much of the research is ambiguous when viewed in the new light. If it is any comfort to do so, one may say that learning has been given a preeminent position in the psychology of personal constructs, even though it has been taken out of circulation as a special topic. In the language of administrators, it has been "kicked upstairs."

Now what happens to the venerable laws of learning and to the family of notions which have more recently grown up in the household of learning? Much! Let us take a look again at what we mean by "construing" and "system." Construing is a way of seeing events that makes them look regular. By construing events it becomes possible to anticipate them. To be effective, the construction system itself must have some regularity. The palpable feature of regularity is repetition, not mere repetition of identical events, of course — in a strict sense that would deny the idea of time its rightful place in the scheme of things — but repetition of some characteristic which can be abstracted from each event and carried intact across the bridge of time and space. To construe is to hear the whisper of recurrent themes in the events that reverberate around us.

The subject in a learning experiment is no exception to our psychological rule. He too directs his psychological processes by seeking the recurrent theme in the experiment. If he segments the experience into separate "trials" and then further separates the "trials" into "reinforced trials" and "unreinforced trials," he may hear the same repetitive theme which the experimenter hears. On the other hand, he may not be so conventional. He may listen for other kinds of themes he has heard before. He may not even segment his experience into the kinds of trials or events the experimenter expects. In the language of music, he may employ another way of phrasing. Viewed in this manner, the problem of learning is not merely one of determining how *many* or what kinds of reinforcements fix a response, or how *many* nonreinforcements extinguish it, but rather, how does the subject phrase the experience, what recurrent themes does he hear, what movements does he define, and what validations of his predictions does he reap? When a subject fails to meet the experimenter's expectations, it may be inappropriate to say that "he has not learned"; rather, one might say that what the subject learned was not what the experimenter expected him to learn. If we are to have a productive science of psychology, let us put the burden of discovery on the experimenter rather than on the subject. Let the experimenter find out what the subject is thinking about, rather than asking the subject to find out what the experimenter is thinking about.

A more adequate discussion of the role of learning in personal-construct theory is reserved for another section on experience presented at a later point in our exposition of the psychology of personal constructs. The present remarks may suffice to suggest the possible extent of the implications of our basic assumptions.

I. Modulation Corollary

22. MODULATION COROLLARY: THE VARIATION IN A PERSON'S CONSTRUCTION SYSTEM IS LIMITED BY THE PERMEABILITY OF THE CONSTRUCTS WITHIN WHOSE RANGE OF CONVENIENCE THE VARIANTS LIE.

If we are to see a person's psychological processes operating lawfully within a system which he constructs, we need also to account for the evolution of the system itself in a similarly lawful manner. Our Experience Corollary states that a person's construction system varies as he successively construes the replications of events. Next, we must note that the progressive variation must, itself, take place within a system. If it were not so, we would be in the position of claiming that little everyday processes are systematically governed but that the system-forming processes are not subordinate to any larger, more comprehensive system. We cannot insist upon the personal lawfulness of the *elements* of human behavior and at the same time concede that the *patterns* of human behavior are unlawful. Nor can we insist that the elements follow a personal system but that the patterns can evolve only within a suprapersonal system.

The problem is a special case of the problem of determinism and free will, which we discussed in an earlier section. There we indicated that we assumed that determination and freedom are two complementary aspects of structure. They cannot exist without each other any more than *up* can exist without *down* or *right* without *left*. Neither freedom nor determination are absolutes. A thing is free *with respect to something;* it is determined *with respect to something else.*

The solution proposed for the problem of determinism and free will provides us with the pattern for understanding how persons can vary and still be considered as lawful phenomena of nature. A person's construction system is composed of complementary superordinate and subordinate relationships. The subordinate systems are determined by the superordinate systems into whose jurisdiction they are placed. The superordinate systems, in turn, are free to invoke new arrangements among the systems which are subordinate to them.

This is precisely what provides for freedom and determination in one's personal construct system. The changes that take place, as one moves toward creating a more suitable system for anticipating events, can be seen as falling under the control of that person's superordinating system. In his role identifying him with his superordinating system, the person is free with respect to subordinate changes he attempts to make. In his role as the follower of his own fundamental principles, he finds his life determined by them. Just as in governmental circles instructions can be changed only within the framework of fixed directives, and directives can be changed only within the framework of fixed statutes, and statutes can be changed only within the framework of fixed constitutions, so can one's personal constructs be changed only within subsystems of constructs and subsystems changed only within more comprehensive systems.

Our position is that even the changes which a person attempts within himself must be construed by him. The new outlook which a person gains from experience is itself an event; and, being an event in his life, it needs to be construed by him if he is to make any sense out of it. Indeed, he cannot even attain the new outlook in the first place unless there is some comprehensive overview within which it can be construed. Another way of expressing the same thing is to say that one does not learn certain things merely from the nature of the stimuli which play upon him; he learns only what his framework is designed to permit him to see in the stimuli.

23. TERMS

a. *Permeability.* Here we introduce a special construct within the psychology of personal constructs which we shall have occasion to use quite frequently in later sections. Particularly in the sections dealing with psychotherapy and the ways of helping persons reconstrue their lives, we shall expect to invoke the notion of *permeability of superordinate constructs.*

A construct is permeable if it will admit to its range of convenience new elements which are not yet construed within its framework. An utterly concrete construct, if there were such a thing, would not be permeable at all, for it would be made up of certain specified elements — those and no others. Such a construct would have to be impermeable.

There are, of course, relative degrees of permeability and impermeability. One person's construct of *good vs. bad* might be sufficiently permeable to permit him to see many new ideas and new acquaintances as good or bad. Another person's construct of *good vs. bad* might include many things but not be open to the inclusion of many new things; most of the good things and most of the bad things have already been labeled — and he has almost run out of labels.

The notion of permeability as a feature of conceptualization stems from the painstaking research of L. S. McGaughran, who approached the problems of conceptualization empirically and inductively. As a result of his investigation he was able to show that certain highly abstracted characteristics of a person's verbal behavior were predictive of his nonverbal behavior when dealing with palpable objects. While he does not use the term in his writings, in a conversation he once did propose the word *permeability* as a symbol for one of the aspects of conceptualization which he had abstracted. For his purposes, he found *permeability* to be a more useful dimension on which to plot conceptualization than the classical *abstract-concrete* dimension.

In our own usage a permeable construct is not necessarily loose, inconsistent, comprehensive, or tenuous. It may be quite definite; it may have little tendency to vary; it may embrace elements which are similar in other ways; and it may be persistently held. When we say that a construct is permeable we refer only to the particular kind of plasticity we have described — the capacity to embrace new elements.

It must be admitted that when new elements are added to the context of a construct there is a tendency for the construct itself to change somewhat. The abstraction of A and B versus C is likely to change when D is taken into consideration. For this reason permeable constructs may show a tendency to shift slightly from time to time. But the shift may be minimal, and shifting is not what we have in mind when we speak of permeability.

In earlier formulations of the theory of personal constructs we used the term "stable aspects" instead of "permeability." Permeable constructs, because they possess resiliency under the impact of new experience, do tend to be stable, but "permeability" is a more precise and operationally useful mark of identification for the kinds of constructs we have in mind than is "stability."

We do not necessarily refer to stability in the sense of longevity or lasting qualities, although a certain permeability in one's constructs gives them durability. Nor do we refer necessarily to a construct's intransigent rigidity in the face of its repeated systematic failures to anticipate events adequately. We refer rather, to those aspects of the system which can span a greater variety of new subordinate variations, which are less shaken by the impact of unexpected minor daily events.

A construct, or an aspect of one's construction system, can be called permeable if it is so constituted that new experience and new events can be discriminatively added to those which it already embraces. A construct which "takes life in its stride" is a permeable one. It is under the regnancy of such constructs that the more subordinate aspects of one's construction system can be systematically varied without making his whole psychological house fall down on him. Sometimes, of course, the house does fall down. Frequently, on a clinical basis, we can see the so-called "decompensation" taking place in a client in the space of a few days or weeks. We are able also to see how the brittleness and impermeability of his construction system failed to support the alterations which he was finding it necessary to make. But more about this later!

The kind of construct which is permeable has more of the qualities of a theoretical formulation, as contrasted with a hypothetical formulation, in science. A hypothesis is deliberately constructed so as to be relatively impermeable and brittle, so that there can be no question about what it embraces and no doubt about its being wholly shattered or left intact at the end of an experiment. A theory is not so inflexibly constructed. It is stated in relatively permeable terms so that it may, in the future, embrace many things which we have not yet thought of. It is stated in an open-ended form. A theory, then, both provokes and accepts a wide variety of experimental ventures, some of which may even be antithetical to each other.

Just as a scientific experimenter's formulations of successive experiments may undergo progressive changes in a manner which is always subordinate to the more theoretical aspects of his system, so any person, scientist or not, may vary his construction system in a manner which is subordinate to certain more permeable aspects of his system. The way the scientist uses his theory to accomplish this is a special case. We have tried, in this corollary, to state the more general case.

b. *Variants.* The constructs which replace each other may be considered to be the variants. Suppose a person starts out with a construct of *fear vs. domination* and shifts it to a construct of *respect vs. contempt.* Whereas once he divided his acquaintances between those he was afraid of and those whom he could dominate, he may, as he grows more mature, divide his acquaintances between those whom he respects and those whom he holds in contempt. But, in order for him to make this shift, he needs another construct, within whose range of convenience the *fear vs. domination* construct lies and which is sufficiently permeable to admit the new idea of *respect vs. contempt.* The two constructs, the old and the new, are the variants.

The permeable construct within whose range of convenience the variants lie may be such a notion as that of *maturity vs. childishness.* The attitude of *fear vs. domination* may be construed as a "childish" notion and the attitude of *respect vs. contempt* may be considered to be a relatively "mature" idea. Or it may be that both old and new constructs are seen as similar with respect to maturity vs. childishness. In the former case the person will see his new attitude as contrasting with the old in this respect; in the latter case he will see the new attitude as essentially similar to the old in this respect.

The psychotherapist who is concerned with his clients' psychological reconstruction of their lives runs across both types of transition in the course of his practice. The essential feature, from the standpoint of the assumptive structure of this theory, is that any transition needs to be subsumed by some overriding construction which is permeable enough to admit the new construct to its context. It is extremely difficult in practice to accomplish extensive psychotherapeutic results in a client whose superordinate structures are impermeable and most of whose basic conceptualizations are rooted exclusively in the past.

The client whose overriding structures are all permeable also presents certain therapeutic problems. Some of the structures which might better have their contexts closed out so that they will not be used to deal with new ideas may cause difficulty for the client as he construes the changes which are taking place in himself. But we are getting ahead of ourselves in this exposition of the psychology of personal constructs! The technical problems in the psychological reconstruction of life are reserved for a later discussion.

J. Fragmentation Corollary

24. FRAGMENTATION COROLLARY: A PERSON MAY SUCCESSIVELY
    EMPLOY A VARIETY OF CONSTRUCTION SUBSYSTEMS WHICH ARE
    INFERENTIALLY INCOMPATIBLE WITH EACH OTHER.

A person's construction system is continually in a state of
flux. Yet, even though it is fluctuating within a superordinate
system, his successive formulations may not be derivable from
each other. It is possible that what Willie thinks today may not
be inferred directly from what he was thinking yesterday. His
shift, nevertheless, in the light of our Modulation Corollary,
is consistent with the more stable aspects of his system. What
we are being careful to say now is that new constructs are not
necessarily direct derivatives of, or special cases within, one's
old constructs. We can be sure only that the changes that
take place from old to new constructs do so within a larger system.

Now those larger systems may have been altered (within a
still greater system, of course) by the impact of the old construct. In that case and in that sense the old construct is a
legitimate precursor of the new construct. The relationship is
still a collateral one, however, rather than a lineal one. The old
and the new constructs may, in themselves, be inferentially incompatible with each other.

This is an important corollary. It should make even clearer
the assumed necessity for seeking out the regnant construct system in order to explain the behavior of men, rather than seeking merely to explain each bit of behavior as a derivative of
its immediately antecedent behavior. If one is to understand
the course of the stream of consciousness, he must do more than
chart its headwaters; he must know the terrain through which
it runs and the volume of the flood which may cut out new
channels or erode old ones.

This is the point where statistical sampling theory may lead
us astray if we are not careful to use it discriminatingly. If we
are making an idiographic study by analyzing a sample of the
population of previous behaviors, we may make the mistake of
assuming that a sample of future behaviors would be drawn

from a universe having exactly the same parameters. From this kind of inference we would be led to believe that a four-year-old child who sucks his thumb fifteen hours a day would grow up to be a man who most likely would suck his thumb about fifteen hours a day. If we turn to sampling theory in a nomothetic framework, we may make another kind of mistake. We may assume that since most men do not suck their thumbs at all, this child will also grow up to be a man who will have no unusual habit of this type.

We are less likely to make a mistake if we are careful to look at the problem in the manner which was suggested in the preceding chapter. If we study the sample of past behaviors and extract our abstraction generalization, not in terms of a quantitative prediction of behaviors of the same order, but rather in terms of an abstraction or regnant construct of those behaviors, we may be able to solve our problem. We may come up with some such answer as the following: a sample of this particular child's behavior appears to be drawn from a population of behavior whose average is fifteen hours of thumb sucking a day. Up to this point we shall have used sampling theory within the idiographic frame. Now let us form a concept. Sampling theory will not help us do that; indeed, there is no reason to expect it to. Let us look at the child's other behaviors in a manner which will enable us to construe them, to form a construct, or, better still, to discover the child's own construction, verbalized or unverbalized, under which these different behaviors emerge. We look at the other behaviors. We sample them also idiographically. Since a construct is a way of seeing some things as being alike and, by the same token, as being different from other things, we shall seek the way in which some of the child's behaviors are alike and at the same time different from other behaviors. To use the common notion of "abstraction," we shall *abstract* his behavior and, possibly, come up with such a construct as "oral behavior," or "ingestive behavior," or "comfort behavior," or "narcissistic behavior." At this second stage in our reasoning process we shall have used concept formation, not sampling theory.

As a third step, let us move over into the nomothetic frame and try out our newly formed construct. Let us see whether it fits other children, whether their behavior can be similarly construed as having elements some of which consistently fall into the category of our construct of oral behavior and others of which clearly do not. Again, this is concept-formation or sorting procedure, not statistical sampling in the ordinary sense.

The fourth step is to see whether the construct fits adult behaviors. Again the framework is nomothetic.

The fifth step is statistical sampling in the nomothetic frame. We see whether or not a sample of childhood behaviors, of the abstract type we have construed, is correlated with a sample of adult behaviors of the same construct type. Presumably we will want to study the same people — as children, then as adults — although, under certain assumptions, we may study the correlation by some indirect method, such as by matching children with adults on some relevant variables which are already known to remain fairly constant throughout life.

Let us note that sampling and concept formation are not wholly different processes, though, for the purposes of the preceding discussion, it was convenient to label them so. In sampling, one makes certain hypotheses (an experimental and a null) as to the way in which two samples are similar, and then tests them.

25. THE PROBLEM OF CONSISTENCY

One of the difficulties which arise in propounding a system like the psychology of personal constructs is that the reader is likely to expect any true construct system to be logic-tight and wholly internally consistent. Yet a candid inspection of our own behavior and our own thinking makes it difficult to see how such an ideal system could exist in reality. Consistency is not an easy concept to handle in a meaningful fashion. What is consistent with what? Is thumb sucking in childhood consistent with thumb sucking in adulthood? Is it consistent with pipe smoking in adulthood? Is it consistent with the accumulation of property? Is it consistent with financial success? Is there anything that it is not consistent with? Is anything inconsistent with anything else?

If everything can be reconciled and made to appear consistent with everything else, the notion of consistency fails to meet our standards for a construct — a way in which at least two things are alike and at the same time different from at least one other thing. If it is not a construct, it cannot help us anticipate events. If it cannot help us anticipate events, it is of no service to science whose goal is prediction. Unless we accord to the notion of consistency a special meaning that gives it the status of a construct, either in the eyes of the person who seeks to reconcile his own behaviors or in the eyes of the observer who seeks to understand those behaviors, the term might better not be relied upon.

Before discussing a particular way of understanding consistency, let us take time to mention the theme of self-consistency that underlies some of the neophenomenological systems of today: Raimy's self-concept theory, Lecky's self-consistency theory, Rogers' client-centered approach, and Snygg and Combs's phenomenal field approach. All of these contemporary theories have enough similarity to personal-construct theory to make it important, from time to time in this discussion, to distinguish their differences as well as their similarities.

Lecky's self-consistency theory treated consistency as if it were a property of the ideas one has. He said that one method of dealing with inconsistency is to try to injure or destroy the objects or persons in connection with which the alien idea arose. Another method is "to reinterpret the disturbing incident in such a manner that it can be assimilated." Another is "to alter the opinion one holds of himself." This all seems reasonable enough, but one soon finds himself wondering what constitutes consistency or inconsistency.

Part of the answer, probably anticipated by Lecky, although he did not express it in so many words, is that consistency and inconsistency are personal labels. What one person sees as inconsistent another may see as consistent. While Lecky was concerned primarily with the problem of consistency and inconsistency of new ideas with the underlying self-idea, his view of consistency per se was that it was a property attributed to experience by the person who has the experience. In our own terms, his "consistency" is a construct, and it is a personal one.

But to say the *consistency-inconsistency* construct is a personal one is not enough to make it applicable. When we hold to two views which are consistent with each other we expect to choose similar, or at least compatible, courses of action under them. The two views are inconsistent if they require us to perform the impossible feat of riding off in opposite directions at the same time. They are inconsistent if they lead us to anticipate two incompatible events. The key to the proper labeling of consistency lies in our Fundamental Postulate: a person's processes are psychologically channelized by the way in which he anticipates events. The operational definition of consistency can be written in terms of the way events are anticipated. Do the wagers one lays on the outcome of life cancel each other out or do they add up?

Our Fragmentation Corollary avers that a person may *successively* employ a variety of construction subsystems which are inferentially incompatible with each other. This means that his subsequent bets on the turn of minor events may not always add up with his earlier bets. Does this mean that his personality is structured only with respect to his minor anticipations? No!

The Fragmentation Corollary is, in part, a derivative of the Modulation Corollary. We said in the latter corollary that the variation in a person's construction system is limited by the permeability of the constructs within whose ranges of convenience the variants lie. We did not assume that variation in a person's constructions is subordinate to all antecedent (in time) aspects of his system. Our assumption is simply that it is in the context of the more permeable aspects of one's system that consistency is the law.

Now that we have suggested a more operational definition of consistency, the intent of the Modulation Corollary should be more clearly communicated. The Fragmentation Corollary follows as an explicit statement of the kind of inconsistency which the Modulation Corollary implicitly tolerates. The Modulation Corollary tolerates inconsistency between subsystems. More specifically, it tolerates the successive use of subsystems which do not, in themselves, add up.

A few sentences back, when we stated that a person's bets on the turn of minor events may not add up with his earlier bets, we asked if this meant that his personality is structured only with respect to his minor anticipations. We gave an emphatic no. Looking at the Fragmentation Corollary in the context of the Modulation Corollary one can give a more comprehensive answer. Now we can say that while a person's bets on the turn of minor events may not appear to add up, his wagers on the outcome of life do tend to add up. He may not win each time, but his wagers, in the larger contexts, do not altogether cancel themselves out. The superordinate permeable features of his system may not be verbalized, they may be more "vegetative" than "spiritual," or they may be seen as what Adler would have called a "style of life"; but they are part of a *system* and, therefore, may be considered from the viewpoint of their lawful as well as from the viewpoint of their free aspects.

As in the case of the idiographic-nomothetic issue, and as in the case of the determinism-free will issue, it is by considering the relative levels of abstraction and generality involved, or the permeability-impermeability levels with which we are dealing, or, in brief, by considering our problem in terms of the individual's personal construct system and the person's attempts to anticipate events, that we are able to come to a satisfactory answer to the important psychological question of how the human organism can be organized and still appear to behave in a disorganized fashion.

26. FURTHER IMPLICATIONS OF THE FRAGMENTATION COROLLARY

Since the variation in a person's construction system is subordinate to certain more permeable aspects of his system, each time his behaviors or his ideas undergo a change he must invoke, in some way or other, the permeable construct which provides the thread of consistency in his behaviors. If that permeable construct is not too clearly patterned, or if it is not too permeable, he may have to abandon its use and seek frantically for new ways of making sense out of life. These frantic attempts at new large concept formation may yield some weirdly new constructs, as he attempts to find the respects in which the events of life have definite likenesses and differences.

There is no clearer example of the limitation of one's ability to adjust to the vicissitudes of life, due to the impermeability of his superordinate constructs, than the case of a compulsion-neurosis client who is undergoing a marked decompensation process. The construct system of such a client is characteristically impermeable; he needs a separate pigeonhole for each new experience and he calculates his anticipations of events with minute pseudomathematical schemes. He has long been accustomed to subsume his principles. The variety of construction subsystems which are inferentially incompatible with each other may, in the train of rapidly moving events, become so vast that he is hard put to it to find ready-made superordinate constructs which are sufficiently permeable or open-ended to maintain over-all consistency. He starts making new ones. While he has very little successful experience with concept formation at the permeable level, these are the kinds of concepts he tries to develop. They may turn out to be generalized suspicions of the motives of other people. They may have to do with reevaluations of life and death. They may lead him to anticipate reality in very bizarre ways.

A person's tolerance of incompatibility in his daily construction of events is also limited by the definition of the regnant constructs upon whose permeability he depends to give life its over-all meaning. If those constructs are so loosely defined that he has trouble getting organized, as in an emotional state, we may see him shifting his behavior pattern back and forth, or reducing it to a childlike pattern which, though not very applicable to the present situation, does appear to provide optimal anticipations at the moment. In this case, too, we see what happens when the permeability and definition of one's superordinate constructs ceases to provide consistency, and the person is thrown back upon a more primitive and less effectual system, albeit a more permeable one.

K. Commonality Corollary

27. COMMONALITY COROLLARY: TO THE EXTENT THAT ONE PERSON EMPLOYS A CONSTRUCTION OF EXPERIENCE WHICH IS SIMILAR TO THAT EMPLOYED BY ANOTHER, HIS PSYCHOLOGICAL PROCESSES ARE SIMILAR TO THOSE OF THE OTHER PERSON.

We come now to a discussion of the implications of our Fundamental Postulate in the field of interpersonal relations. As we have already indicated, it is possible for two people to be involved in the same real events but, because they construe them differently, to experience them differently. Since they construe them differently, they will anticipate them differently and will behave differently as a consequence of their anticipations. That there should be such differences seems to be a logical outcome of our Fundamental Postulate, and we have stated that fact in the Individuality Corollary. But if we have an Individuality Corollary, we must also have a Commonality Corollary.

As with the other corollaries the Commonality Corollary is little more than a clarification of what seems to be implicit in our Fundamental Postulate. If a person's processes are psychologically channelized by the ways in which he anticipates events, and if he anticipates events by construing their replications, it may seem obvious that we are assuming that, if two persons employed the same construction of experience, their psychological processes would have to duplicate each other. This seems like an innocent statement. But as we examine this corollary closely, we find it has some implications which are not generally accepted among psychologists.

It is important to make clear that we have not said that if one person has experienced the same events as another he will duplicate the other's psychological processes. This is the assumption of stimulus-response psychology and, in its way, a perfectly respectable assumption; but it is not our assumption, and because we have not chosen to make it, we are free to develop our theoretical position in ways in which the stimulus-response psychologist is not. We could say, with systematic consistency, that two persons with identical experience would have identical psychological processes. But such a statement might be misleading unless the reader kept clearly in mind just what we mean by *experience*. He might have to keep turning back to our discussion of the Experience Corollary to see wherein our position differs from that of stimulus-response theory. So we prefer to state it the way we have — that two persons' psychological processes will be as similar as their constructions of experience.

One of the advantages of this position is that it does not require us to assume that it would take identical events in the lives of two people to make them act alike. Two people can act alike even if they have each been exposed to quite different phenomenal stimuli. It is in the similarity in the construction of events that we find the basis for similar action, and not in the identity of the events themselves. Again, as in the matter of learning, we think the psychologist can better understand his subjects if he inquires into the way in which they construe their stimuli than if he always takes his own construction of the stimuli for granted. In the words of our Modulation Corollary, we think psychologists need to use more permeable constructs in their own systems so that they can better subsume the variant constructions of their subjects.

Phenomenologically speaking, no two persons can have either the same construction or the same psychological processes. In that sense our Commonality Corollary would be unrealistic. But what we mean is this: to the extent that we can construe the constructions of two other people as being similar, we may anticipate that their psychological processes may also be construed as similar.

28. TERMS

a. *To the extent.* In our Individuality Corollary we committed ourselves to the view that persons differ from each other in their constructions of events. The Commonality Corollary may appear to imply a contradiction to this previous statement. But when we say that persons differ from each other we do not rule out the possibility that there may be certain respects in which persons can be construed as being like each other. To say that James differs from John is not to say that James and John have nothing in common. In fact, to say that two things differ from each other in every conceivable respect is to express the ultimate in particularism and to leave one's listener in a confused state of mind about the whole matter. It is also about as confusing to say that two things are like each other in every conceivable respect; one is left wondering how they can then be considered as two distinct things.

What we have said in our Commonality Corollary does not contradict what we have assumed in our Individuality Corollary. By using the term, *to the extent,* we indicate that we are designating a totality of aspects in which the two persons' constructions of experience may be construed as similar. That there will still be many respects in which the two persons will retain their individuality goes without saying — our Individuality Corollary took care of that.

b. *Construction of experience.* Experience, as we have defined it, is a matter of successively construing events. To construe experience, then, is to take stock of the outcome of this successive construing process. Thus, if two people take similar stock of their successive interpretations, their behavior will exhibit similar characteristics. The historical development of their thinking need not be similar — only the stock-taking need be similar. Hence it is not the similarity of experience which provides the basis for similarity of action, but similarity of their present construction of that experience.

By construction of experience we do not necessarily refer to highly verbalized interpretations. We keep reiterating this point. A person may construe his experience with little recourse to words, as, for example, in certain conditioned reflexes. Even those constructions which are symbolized by words are not necessarily similar just because the words are similar. Conversely, two persons may be using essentially the same constructions of their experience, although they express themselves in quite different terms.

29. IMPLICATIONS OF THE COMMONALITY COROLLARY

It is an observed fact that certain groups of people behave similarly in certain respects. Some of these similarities are associated with similarities in their ages, some with similarities in what is expected of them by their associates, some with similarities in experience, and some with other kinds of constructions of similarity. Indeed, if we wish, we can approach the matter of similarities between persons from any one of a number of angles.

One of the common and interesting approaches to similarities and differences between persons is that taken from the standpoint of culture. Usually, as the term "culture" would imply, this means that we see persons grouped according to similarities in their upbringing and their environment. This, basically, means that cultural similarities and differences are understood in terms of stimulus-response theory.

Sometimes, however, culture is taken to mean similarity in what members of the group expect of each other. This is an interpretation of culture which is more commonly found among sociological than among psychological theories. Psychologists perhaps avoid this approach because it seems to require that one interpret the behavior of more than one person at a time; they prefer an approach which permits them to derive their system from observations of the individual man.

When one does understand culture in terms of similarity of expectations, he can proceed from that point in one of two directions. He can consider the expectations of others as stimuli to which each person is subjected; or he can understand cultural similarity between persons as essentially a similarity in what they perceive is expected of them. The latter approach throws the emphasis back upon the outlook of the individual person. This is, of course, the kind of approach one would be expected to make if he employed the psychology of personal constructs.

The similarity-of-expectations view of culture is also consistent with personal-construct theory from another angle. Our Fundamental Postulate assumes that a person's psychological processes are channelized by the ways in which he anticipates events. That makes the psychology of personal constructs an anticipatory theory of behavior. Some of the real events that one anticipates are the behaviors of other persons. Personal-construct theory would then understand cultural similarity, not only in terms of personal outlook rather than in terms of the impingement of social stimuli, but also in terms of what the individual anticipates others will do and, in turn, what he thinks they are expecting him to do.

In interpreting social behavior we are confronted with a spiraliform model. James anticipates what John will do. James also anticipates what John thinks he, James, will do. James further anticipates what John thinks he expects John will do. In addition, James anticipates what John thinks James expects John to predict that James will do. And so on! We are reminded of the famous illustration of the cat looking in the mirror. In complicated social situations, as in psychotherapy, for example, one may find himself looking at another person through such an infinite series of reflections.

Personal-construct theory approaches problems of the commonality of behavior primarily from the point of view of the individual person. Furthermore, it sees his point of view as an anticipatory one. It follows, then, that our approach to culture and group behavior is via the study of similarities and contrasts in a person's anticipations and the channels he constructs for making his predictions. We are interested, not only in the similarities in what people predict, but also in the similarities in their manner of arriving at their predictions. People belong to the same cultural group, not merely because they behave alike, nor because they expect the same things of others, but especially because they construe their experience in the same way. It is on this last similarity that the psychology of personal constructs throws its emphasis.

L. Sociality Corollary

30. SOCIALITY COROLLARY: TO THE EXTENT THAT ONE PERSON CONSTRUES THE CONSTRUCTION PROCESSES OF ANOTHER, HE MAY PLAY A ROLE IN A SOCIAL PROCESS INVOLVING THE OTHER PERSON.

While a common or similar cultural background tends to make people see things alike and to behave alike, it does not guarantee cultural progress. It does not even guarantee social harmony. The warriors who sprang up from the dragon's teeth sown by Jason had much in common but, misconstruing each other's motives, they failed to share in a constructive enterprise and soon destroyed each other. In order to play a constructive role in relation to another person one must not only, in some measure, see eye to eye with him but must, in some measure, have an acceptance of him and of his way of seeing things. We say it in another way: the person who is to play a constructive role in a social process with another person need not so much construe things as the other person does as he must effectively construe the other person's outlook.

Here we have a take-off point for a social psychology. By attempting to place at the forefront of psychology the understanding of personal constructs, and by recognizing, as a corollary of our Fundamental Postulate, the subsuming of other people's construing efforts as the basis for social interaction, we have said that social psychology must be a psychology of interpersonal understandings, not merely a psychology of common understandings.

There are different levels at which we can construe what other people are thinking. In driving down the highway, for example, we stake our lives hundreds of times a day on our accuracy in predicting what the drivers of the oncoming cars will do. The orderly, extremely complex, and precise weaving of traffic is really an amazing example of people predicting each other's behavior through subsuming each other's perception of a situation. Yet actually each of us knows very little about the higher motives and the complex aspirations of the oncoming drivers, upon whose behavior our own lives depend. It is enough, for the purpose of avoiding collisions, that we understand or subsume only certain specific aspects of their construction systems. If we are to understand them at higher levels, we must stop traffic and get out to talk with them.

If we can predict accurately what others will do, we can adjust ourselves to their behavior. If others know how to tell what we will do, they can adjust themselves to our behavior and may give us the right of way. This mutual adjustment to each other's viewpoint takes place, in the terms of the theory of personal constructs, because, to some extent, our construction system subsumes the construction systems of others and theirs, in part, subsume ours. Understanding does not have to be a one-way proposition; it can be mutual.

For the touch and go of traffic it is not necessary for the motorists to have an extensive mutual understanding of each other's ways of seeing things but, within a restricted range and at the concrete level of specific acts represented by traffic, the mutual understandings must be precise. For the more complicated interplay of roles — for example, for the husband-and-wife interplay — the understanding must cover the range of domestic activities at least, and must reach at least a level of generality which will enable the participants to predict each other's behavior in situations not covered by mere household traffic rules.

One person may understand another better than he is understood. He may understand more of the other's ways of looking at things. Moreover, he may understand the other at a higher level of generality. Presumably, if this is true of a certain person with respect to a group of people whose ways of seeing things have some commonality, he is in a strategic position to assume a leadership relationship to the group. On the other hand, there may be still other factors which effectively deny him that opportunity.

A therapist-client relationship is one which exemplifies greater understanding on the part of one member than on the part of the other. As a therapist comes to subsume the client's construction system within his own, he becomes more and more facile in developing his own role in relation to the client. It then becomes possible for them to make progress jointly in a social enterprise.

Parenthetically it should be admitted that the therapist-client relationship can, in some instances, be effective with the client's understanding more about the therapist's construction system than the therapist understands about the client's. Some therapists conduct their interviews with so much elaboration of their own views that this kind of role relationship might easily be the outcome. Some clients try to manage the interplay of roles so that they can find out what the therapist thinks — as if that would help them get along in life — without letting the therapist in on what they think. If he accepts the flattery, the therapist may waste time confiding his views to the client.

Perhaps somewhat more legitimately, the therapist, in his relationship with the client, may carefully manage his own role and the constructions of experience which he permits the client to observe. In that way he may enable the client to develop a role under certain presumptions about the therapist. The therapist may tentatively present a carefully calculated point of view in such a way that the client, through coming to understand it, may develop a basis for understanding other figures in his environment with whom he needs to acquire skill in playing interacting roles. This is known as *role playing* in psychotherapy and there are many ways in which it may be effectively employed.

31. DEFINITION OF ROLE

In terms of the theory of personal constructs, a *role* is a psychological process based upon the role player's construction of aspects of the construction systems of those with whom he attempts to join in a social enterprise. In less precise but more familiar language, a role is an ongoing pattern of behavior that follows from a person's understanding of how the others who are associated with him in his task think. In idiomatic language, a role is a position that one can play on a certain team without even waiting for the signals.

This definition of *role* lays emphasis upon several important points. First, like other patterns of behavior, it is assumed to be tied to one's personal construct system. This implies that it is anchored in the outlook of the role player and does not necessarily follow from his congregate relationship to other members of a group. It is a pattern of behavior emerging from the person's own construction system rather than primarily out of his social circumstances. He plays out his part in the light of his understanding of the attitudes of his associates, even though his understanding may be minimal, fragmentary, or misguided. This notion of role is, therefore, neither a typical stimulus-response notion nor a typical sociological notion. We believe it is essentially consistent with our Fundamental Postulate and with the various corollaries which have already been stated.

The second point to be emphasized is that this definition of role is not equivalent to the "self-concept" as used in some psychological systems. Seeing oneself as playing a role is not equivalent to identifying oneself as a static entity; but rather, as throughout the theory of personal constructs, the role refers to a process — an ongoing activity. It is that activity carried out in relation to, and with a measure of understanding of, other people that constitutes the role one plays.

The third point to be emphasized is that this definition ties up the role with a social process. While the concept of role is appropriate to a psychological system which is concerned with individual persons, it is defined herein so that it is dependent upon cognate developments within a group of two or more people. It is not enough that the role player organize his behavior with an eye on what other people are thinking; he must be a participant, either in concert or in opposition, within a group movement. This further restriction of the definition of a role places emphasis upon team membership on the part of the role player.

The fourth point to be emphasized is that, while one person may play a role in a social process involving the other person, through subsuming a version of that other person's way of seeing things, the understanding need not be reciprocated. Thus the one person is playing a role in a social process, but the other is not playing a role in that social process. This is the way we have chosen to define *role*. It does not mean that the other person is not a factor to be taken into account in explaining the social process.

The fifth and final point to be emphasized is that this definition of role does not insist upon commonality in the construct systems of the people involved in the social process or in the persons specifically involved in playing roles. Commonality between construction systems may make it more likely that one construction system can subsume a part of another, but that fact is incidental rather than essential in those cases where roles are played between people who think alike and understand each other. Moreover, commonality can exist between two people who are in contact with each other without either of them being able to understand the other well enough to engage in a social process with him. The commonality may exist without those perceptions of each other which enable the people to understand each other or to subsume each other's mental processes. As in the case in psychotherapy in which the clinician identifies himself so closely with his client's way of seeing things that he cannot subsume the client's mental processes, the role the clinician plays becomes impoverished and the social process or the productive outcome of the clinician-client relationship comes to a standstill. The management of both transference and countertransference in psychotherapy is an example of the development of roles for both client and therapist.

We have made the point that for people to be able to understand each other it takes more than a similarity or commonality in their thinking. In order for people to get along harmoniously with each other, each must have some understanding of the other. This is different from saying that each must understand things in the same way as the other, and this delicate point has profound implications in psychotherapy. To the extent that people understand each other or, stated in the language of our theory, to the extent that their construction systems subsume each other, their activities in relation to each other may be called *roles*, a role being a course of activity which is played out in the light of one's understanding of the behavior of one or more other people.

Let us make sure, further, that we have not slighted the point that there is a difference between two people's holding the same construction system and two people's understanding each other so that they can play roles in relation to each other. Consider the differences in the characteristic approaches to life of men and women. None of us would claim, we believe, that men and women construe all aspects of life in the same way. And yet nature has provided us with no finer example of role relationships and constructive social interaction than in the sexes. If we look at the testimony of nature, we shall have to admit that it often takes a man to understand a woman and a woman to understand a man and there is no greater tragedy than the failure to arrive at those understandings which permit this kind of role interrelationship.

32. THE LEADERSHIP ROLE

It is not intended to discuss all the implications of the Sociality Corollary at this point. However, it may be helpful to look at certain of its implications in order to suggest what impact this assumption might have in the field of psychology. For example, the Sociality Corollary has implications for the psychology of leadership which may prove useful. It will be necessary, however, first to clarify what is meant by "leadership." In studying groups sociometrically it appears that nominators may make their selections of "leaders" quite differently, depending upon their understanding of what the situation demands. If ingenuity and originality appear to him to be required, a nominator may choose one person. If defense of the group against an outside threat or a superordinate authority is believed to be needed, quite another kind of person may be chosen. If devotion to duty and housekeeping activities are required, still another may be selected. If individual members of the group are afraid their own freedom of action may be constricted if the group becomes tightly organized along certain lines, they may choose as leaders those who promise optimal permissiveness in the group structure. If the nominators feel keenly their interdependence upon each other, and therefore wish to mobilize the group, they may choose still another type of leader.

While prestige or status may be common to nearly all leadership, the psychologist will be badly fooled if he overlooks the variety of leadership patterns because they hold this one feature in common. A leader is one who performs any one of the variety of jobs which are popularly recognized as leadership jobs. He may do the job because of the expectancies with which he is surrounded; in that case, he may "perform better than he is able." Again, he may do the job with such originality that his "leadership" is recognized only in the pages of history.

Let us consider first what is involved in the leadership role of the mobilizing or rallying type of leader. The situation within which he operates tends to accelerate the social processes of the group as a whole, though it sometimes retards the social processes of subgroups or superordinate groups. The rallying leader's contribution to the acceleration of the group's social progress is dependent upon and proportional to his understanding of the relevant features in his colleagues' personal construct systems. By "understanding" we do not mean that he necessarily holds the common viewpoint, but rather that he has a way of looking at his colleagues' ideas that makes sense and enables him to predict their behavior. Of course, a commonality of viewpoint may, to a certain extent, make it easier for him to subsume parts of the construction systems of his colleagues within his own, but commonality is not a necessary prerequisite to subsuming.

Simply stated, the point is that one does not have to be like certain people in order to understand them, but he does have to understand them in certain respects in order to rally them. While this sentence may require some additional modifiers, it does express the central theme of what the psychology of personal constructs has to say about the rallying type of leadership.

In a somewhat different sense the Sociality Corollary provides inferences regarding other types of leadership. The ingenuity leader may not be playing a role in a social process, as we have defined *role* here, but the people who select him may be playing roles in a social process which involves him. In choosing him they are anticipating his contribution to the group and subsuming it within their own constructions of the part he ought to play.

The defending leader may not be called upon to perform an intragroup role; his role in a social process is played out primarily in relation to persons outside the group. The housekeeping leader may or may not be playing a role in the sense we have defined it. On the one hand, he may, like the ingenuity leader, be the one in relation to whom others play out their own roles in a social process. On the other hand, he may, as in the case of an effective executive secretary of an organization, understand the explicit and implicit policies of the group so well that he is able, without specific mandate, to act in each newly arising situation just as the group would want him to act.

The compromise leader need not play a role as we have defined it, and the role value of the participation of the people who select him may be minimal. Since his selection implies a slowing down of social process in the particular group with which his leadership is identified, perhaps so that other social processes will not be stifled, it is expected that his role will be constricted. To be sure, as some vice-presidents have done, he may surprise his electors and play out a role which generates more social progress than they bargained for.

33. TESTING THE THEORY OF PERSONAL CONSTRUCTS

Since a theory is an ad interim construction system which is designed to give an optimal anticipation of events, its life is limited by its period of usefulness. If this theory proves to be fertile in providing us with testable hypotheses and in suggesting new approaches to the problems psychologists face, it will have cleared its first hurdle. If, subsequently, it occurs that a considerable proportion of the hypotheses prove to be true, and many of the new approaches provide desired control over psychological events, the theory will have reached maturity. When its place is eventually taken by a more comprehensive, a more explicit, a more fertile and more useful theory, it will be time to relegate it to history.

It cannot be expected that we can accomplish any more than the partial clearing of the first hurdle in this presentation. An attempt will be made to show that the theory does provide us with some interesting new approaches to the problems psychologists face, particularly in the field of psychotherapy. Some hypotheses which are believed to be testable by more formal procedures will also be suggested. The establishment of real fertility in this respect, however, will depend upon what the readers of this manuscript come up with as a result of reading it.

M. Summary of Assumptive Structure

34. FUNDAMENTAL POSTULATE AND ITS COROLLARIES

a. *Fundamental Postulate:* A person's processes are psychologically channelized by the ways in which he anticipates events.

b. *Construction Corollary:* A person anticipates events by construing their replications.

c. *Individuality Corollary:* Persons differ from each other in their constructions of events.

d. *Organization Corollary:* Each person characteristically evolves, for his convenience in anticipating events, a construction system embracing ordinal relationships between constructs.

e. *Dichotomy Corollary:* A person's construction system is composed of a finite number of dichotomous constructs.

f. *Choice Corollary:* A person chooses for himself that alternative in a dichotomized construct through which he anticipates the greater possibility for extension and definition of his system.

g. *Range Corollary:* A construct is convenient for the anticipation of a finite range of events only.

h. *Experience Corollary:* A person's construction system varies as he successively construes the replications of events.

i. *Modulation Corollary:* The variation in a person's construction system is limited by the permeability of the constructs within whose ranges of convenience the variants lie.

j. *Fragmentation Corollary:* A person may successively employ a variety of construction subsystems which are inferentially incompatible with each other.

k. *Commonality Corollary:* To the extent that one person employs a construction of experience which is similar to that employed by another, his psychological processes are similar to those of the other person.

l. *Sociality Corollary:* To the extent that one person construes the construction processes of another, he may play a role in a social process involving the other person.

Chapter Three

The Nature of Personal Constructs

WE TURN now to a descriptive elaboration of the psychology of personal constructs in an attempt to give greater palpability to what we have been saying earlier in abstract terms.

A. Personal Usage of Constructs

1. THE BASIC NATURE OF A CONSTRUCT

A construct is a way in which some things are construed as being alike and yet different from others. We have departed from conventional logic by assuming that the construct is just as pertinent to some of the things which are seen as different as it is to the things which are seen as alike. For example, suppose a person construes in terms of a *black vs. white* construct. His field comprises a number of things. Some of them, such as his shirt, his shoes, his house, the paper on which he writes, the skin of his neighbor, and so on, are amenable to the *black vs. white* construct. The construct may be misapplied; he may call his shirt white when his wife sees it as black. It may be inappropriate; merely to construe his neighbor's skin as black may not be a very enlightened way to look at his neighbor. But, all in all, the construct is applicable to those things which for him can be either black or white. Yet there are other things in the person's life. There is the time of day, his affection for his children, the distance to his office, and so on, for which the *black vs. white* construct is patently irrelevant.

a. *Bipolar nature of constructs.* Now conventional logic would say that *black* and *white* should be treated as separate concepts. Moreover, it would say that the opposite of *black* can only be stated as *not black,* and the opposite of *white* can only be stated as *not white.* Thus the person whose field we mentioned would have shoes which would be just as much *not white* as the time of day, and he would write on paper which would be just as *not black* as the distance to his office.

Some logicians take the further view that a concept is a way in which certain things are naturally alike and that all other things are really different. For them the concept is a feature of the nature of the things with which it is concerned and not an interpretative act of someone. We would agree that the concept is real, but its reality exists in its actual employment by its user, and not in the things which it is supposed to explain.

The conventional logic to which we have referred is perfectly respectable in its way. It is an approach to thinking which, for some centuries now, many careful thinkers have assumed to be a good one. Our view would admit it as one of the possible approaches to the problems of psychology. We would not admit that it is nature's ultimate revelation. In a manner which is compatible with the view of constructive alternativism, upon which the psychology of personal constructs is based, we have chosen, for the time being, to abandon the classical notion of concepts and to assume a somewhat different structure of thought. While it is not absolutely necessary that one start out by defending the plausibility of his assumptions, our assumptions regarding the nature of constructs seem to correspond more closely to observation of how persons actually think than do the customary assumptions regarding conceptualization.

b. *Lyle's study.* While our view of constructs as dichotomous abstractions is in the nature of an assumption, and hence not something which needs to be tested within the framework of our theory, there is already some research evidence which supports the view. Lyle, in a study of selective perception, from the standpoint of the psychology of personal constructs, had occasion to factor analyze certain accuracy scores made by subjects who were asked to categorize groups of words. The categories were set up in terms of constructs commonly used by the population from which the sample of subjects was drawn. The list of words was carefully chosen and pretested in order to provide certain controls. These words were then presented to his subjects and they were asked to assign each word to one of the eight categories or to a ninth, or "don't know," category. This was done under pressure of time, with a paced presentation.

Subjects were scored in terms of their accuracy in identifying words "correctly" in each of the eight category groups. "Correct" categorizations were based on agreement in a separately drawn sample of the same population of undergraduate college women. Since each subject produced eight accuracy scores, the data could be factor analyzed.

Lyle's eight categories were chosen so as to represent four construct dimensions: *cheerful vs. sad, broad-minded vs. narrow-minded, refined vs. vulgar,* and *sincere vs. insincere.* However, as far as the selection of words to fit these categories and the experimental presentation were concerned, they were treated as entirely independent concepts.

The factor analysis produced five factors: a general factor which might be called verbal facility, intelligence, or something of the sort, and four factors each of which had a pair of heavy loadings on the contrasting ends of the original construct dimensions. While there was nothing in the selection of terms or in the mathematical procedure which would make the loadings pair off in this manner, it did happen that when persons made errors in assigning terms to Lyle's *cheerful* category they also tended to make errors in assigning terms to his *sad* category, but they did not necessarily make errors in connection with his *broad-minded, narrow-minded, refined, vulgar, sincere,* and *insincere* categories. In a similar manner the other pairs of terms showed up on the loadings of the other factors. This suggests that if *cheerful* corresponds to a construct in a person's personal construct system, its antonym does also. Or, stated in other terms, if a person's personal construct of *cheerful* makes sense in a public system, his personal construct of *sad* will also make sense in the public system. This is what one would expect if one's personal constructs were essentially dichotomous. It is not what one would expect if the concepts of *cheerful* and *sad* were independently abstracted by the person.

Following is Lyle's factor table:

Terms	Factors				
	I	II	III	IV	V
Cheerful	52	6)*	01	02	−03
Sad	47	66*	−03	−04	22
Broad-minded	66	00	42*	05	12
Narrow-minded	72	−02	57*	03	04
Sincere	12	06	−10	75*	02
Insincere	27	−01	12	48*	−05
Refined	00	−04	−07	20	55*
Vulgar	43	03	23	−06	72*

* Indicates highest pair of loadings on each of the specific factors.

c. *Personal range of convenience.* From our point of view, each construct, as used by a person, has a limited range of convenience. Outside that range the person does not find it relevant, one way or the other, to the objects located there. For example, the time of day is an element most people would place outside the range of convenience of their personal construct of *black vs. white*. But within the range of convenience of the construct there is a relevant similarity and difference which together form the essence of the construct. The difference is not simply the outer boundary of relevance of the construct — that boundary is the limit of the range of convenience. Rather, the difference exists within the range of convenience, and it is just as important to the construct as is the similarity.

The elements lying within the range of convenience of the construct are said to constitute its context. For one person the construct of *black vs. white* may have a somewhat different context than for another. For example, one person may classify his moods as black or white, another may classify his fabrications as black or white, and another may use the construct to distinguish between cultures. Moreover, a person who frequently reads the dark-faced type and light-faced type in a railroad time schedule may come to deal even with the time of day within the range of convenience of his *black vs. white* construct. Finally, one person may classify as white what another, perhaps from a different cultural group, classifies as black. For example, in European cultural groups black is the color of mourning, while in parts of the Orient white is the color used to symbolize grief.

d. *Usefulness of the dichotomous assumption.* Have dichotomous construction systems proved useful in the field of science? This is an important question to ask, for we are ascribing a dichotomous quality to all human thinking. It is therefore quite relevant to ask whether or not previous attempts to ascribe dichotomy to phenomena have proved valuable.

Let us cite two cases in which dichotomous thinking has proved to be particularly useful. The first is in the field of electromagnetism, and later, electronics. Here the notion of positive and negative poles and charges has opened the door to many important discoveries and inventions. Yet the notion of *positive vs. negative* is only an assumption which was imposed upon the data; the atoms did not come around to the scientists and ask to be divided into positive and negative aspects. The second outstanding example of the successful use of dichotomy is Mendel's theory of genes. While no one has yet been able to point to a palpable gene of either the dominant or recessive type, the concept of *dominant vs. recessive* has proved to be remarkably fruitful.

It is important for us to keep in mind that it is not the accumulation of the elements in the context that constitutes the construct, nor is it the differential grouping of the elements. Rather, the construct is the *basis* upon which elements are understood. It is a matter of how the person construes the elements in order to deal with them, not where they happen to appear or where he decides to set them down. The construct is an interpretation of a situation and is not itself the situation which it interprets.

Our view of constructs makes it appear that all people's thinking must be abstract, and never absolutely concrete. We assume that is true. We do not envision the possibility of an entirely concrete psychological response. Even perception, long thought to be something quite different from conceptualization, is assumed to be an act of construing. But we do see some individuals who are much more concretistic in their outlooks than are others. They have difficulty making the bridge from element to element unless the elements are laid physically side by side. But even so, they must abstract the elements in some degree, else their lives would be hopelessly kaleidoscopic and there would be no possibility of internal organization.

2. DO PEOPLE MEAN WHAT THEY SAY?

It is not possible for one to express the whole of his construction system. Many of one's constructs have no symbols to be used as convenient word handles. They are therefore difficult, not only for others to grasp and subsume within their own systems, but also difficult for the person himself to manipulate or to subsume within the verbally labeled parts of his system. The fact that they do not readily lend themselves to organization within the verbally labeled parts of the system makes it difficult for a person to be very articulate about how he feels, or for him to predict what he will do in a future situation which, as yet, exists only in terms of verbal descriptions.

A person may say that he will not take a drink if he is offered one tomorrow. But when he says so he is aware only of what he can verbally label; he is not fully aware of what it will be like tomorrow when tomorrow's situation actually confronts him. The situation which he envisions is, to be sure, one in which he would not take the drink. But the situation which actually rolls around may loom up quite differently and he may do what he has promised himself and others he would not do. There may be a failure of his structure, or, more particularly, that part of it which is verbally labeled, to subsume adequately certain aspects of the rest of the system.

There is another respect in which it may appear that one does not mean what he says. It may be impossible for one to express certain constructs in such a way that others can subsume them within their own systems without mispredicting him. They "take him at his word," but he does not mean by his word what they think he means. It therefore appears that he does not mean what he says. Sometimes a person's verbal expression represents such a contamination of constructs that he himself, when he hears a transcription of his remarks against a different background of circumstances, may be amazed at what then seems to be the import of his verbal behavior. This happens in psychotherapy when a client hears transcriptions of parts of earlier interviews.

a. *Incomplete expression.* Often people express their constructs incompletely. Let us keep in mind that a construct is a way in which some things are alike and yet different from others. In its minimum context a construct would be a way in which two things are alike and different from a third. It should be kept in mind that the *way* in which the two things are like each other should be the same as the *way* in which they are different from the third. We do not explicitly express a whole construct if we say, "Mary and Alice have gentle dispositions but neither of them is as attractive as Jane." We would have to say something like this, if we were to express a true construct: "Mary and Alice are gentle; Jane is not." Or we might say, "Jane is more attractive than Mary or Alice."

When we say, "Mary and Alice have gentle dispositions but neither of them is as attractive as Jane," we may be implying two different constructs: *gentleness* and *attractiveness.* The selection of an adjective to describe two persons, or even to describe one person, usually means that the speaker has formed a category which, for him, has the simultaneous inclusive and exclusive properties of a construct. To say that Mary is gentle is to imply that at least one other person is gentle also and that at least one other person is not gentle. Or it may imply that at least two other persons are not gentle.

The minimum context for a construct is *three* things. We

cannot express a construct, either explicitly or implicitly, without involving at least two things which have a likeness and one which is, by the same token, different. To say that Mary and Alice are "gentle" and not imply that somewhere in the world there is someone who is "not gentle" is illogical. More than that, it is unpsychological.

Now a person may be heard to say, "Mary and Alice are gentle and I cannot conceive of anyone's not being gentle." Such a speaker may be attempting to avoid placing himself in the position of one who sees ungentleness. His statement may thus provide an important lead for the psychologist who is seeking to understand him. On the other hand, the speaker may be restricting the reference of the concept to the idiographic frame. He may, if we ask him, indicate that he means, "Mary and Alice are gentle *now*, as contrasted with some other time" — in other words, that gentleness is not a construct which distinguishes people from each other, but rather one which distinguishes day-to-day variation in persons. This construction of gentleness may also throw considerable light upon the speaker's own pattern of day-to-day mood changes. It is certainly profitable to listen carefully to a speaker's use of constructs.

Sometimes a person will attempt to limit the context to two things which are unlike in some way. He may say, "Mary is gentle; Jane is not. I know of no one else who is like either of them." It may be a little more difficult to see, but this also represents a verbal distortion of conceptualization. Mary and Jane have already been distinguished when they entered the discussion identified by their names. To say that they are further distinguished by their gentleness or lack of it is to add nothing to the distinction, unless that further distinction, by indicating a kinship of at least one of them with a third person, classifies them. While this kind of conceptual distortion is not as common as that described in the previous paragraph, it does indicate that the speaker is having trouble communicating the kinship he covertly construes between Mary and Jane and the other people in his social world. The missing *like* element in the expression of his construct is quite possibly denied because he himself is it. To say that his conceptualization of Mary and Jane is concretistic is not enough; he is really in trouble about Mary and Jane.

One cannot help but be reminded, at this point, of those psychologists and others who insist that everyone is an "individual" and that we cannot understand one individual through understanding other individuals. Here is a form of conceptual distortion which seems to betray the particular scientist's deeply rooted confusion about what to do about "people." The therapist who is really reduced to this sort of reasoning is likely to find that his therapeutic efforts extract a heavy toll from him, and the problem of transference and countertransference (because he himself covertly becomes one of the two missing figures in the constructural context) is one which he cannot face. The insistence upon the exclusive use of the idiographic frame is a further example of the attempt to reduce all social constructs to a context comprised solely of unlikenesses. That mistake, at least, is one which is avoided in the psychology of personal constructs by the recognition that the abstractions which are lifted from a sample of behaviors of a single person may, in turn, be used as data from which abstractions are lifted from a sample of people of a group.

We have spoken of the two types of instances in which a speaker may attempt to limit the context of his construct to two things: the first in which he attempts to limit the context to two or more *like* things, and the second in which he attempts to limit the context to two or more *unlike* things. Next let us consider the case in which he attempts to limit the context to one thing only.

"Mary is gentle. I wouldn't say that anyone else was gentle and I wouldn't say that they weren't." This is not even equivalent to the redundant statement that "Mary is Mary." By calling a person "Mary," we are at least implying that all of her is "Mary" and that other people are "not Mary." But the speaker who says that Mary is gentle but still insists that gentleness provides neither kinship nor distinction for Mary is failing to communicate a construct. It may be, of course, that he means that

Mary is gentle now *like* she was at some other time and *unlike* she was at still a third time. More likely, he is unable to bring himself to the point of full expression of his construct. At the verbal level, at least, his construct has probably reached the point of complete impermeability. He is not in a position to use it for meeting new situations in life or for readjusting to old. He cannot organize other constructs under it. On the verbal level, the construct has become inoperative.

b. *Names as personal construct symbols.* Are proper names expressions of constructs? Yes. A name is a way of seeing a likeness in one group of events which distinguishes it from another group of events. Over here, we have a group of events which may be seen as being alike by way of being "Mary events." Over there are the events, still within the range of convenience of the construct, which are "un-Mary-like events." "Mary" is a construct of events. So, any name is a kind of construction of events. This is a partial answer to critics of Raimy's self-concept theory who, on logical grounds, claim that the term "self-concept" is a misnomer; that it should be called "self-percept" or "self-identity." In terms of classical logic, these critics are, of course, correct in their criticism. However, in terms of our functional definition of construct and our theoretical position in the psychology of personal constructs, it is quite appropriate to refer to a given person's self-construct, or to a class of constructs which can be called personal self-constructs.

c. *Nondiscriminating universals.* Finally, let us look at the instance in which an attempt is made to express a universal similarity. "Mary, Alice, Jane, and everyone else are always gentle." This reminds one of the common expression, "Everything is good." Taken literally, both statements deny their constructs. If everyone is gentle, the construct of gentleness has no meaning. But the speaker must mean something. The listener must look beyond the literal symbolism and construe the speaker's personal construction.

There are several possibilities. Suppose the contrast to "gentleness" in the speaker's system is something we might call "aggressiveness." If the speaker says that "everyone is gentle," he avoids pointing to anyone and labeling him "aggressive." He may do this because he does not want to be in the position of one who is known as a seer of aggressiveness. He may do it because he cannot deal satisfactorily with aggressive people and, for the moment at least, is trying to limit his population to people he can deal with. Then there may be an implied exception in the statement; he may mean, "Everyone *except me* is gentle." Another interpretation is that he may feel that if anyone in the world is aggressive it would have to be himself, his own latent aggression is so great. The only way, therefore, that he can escape being the prime example of aggressiveness is to insist that everyone is gentle.

A similar interpretation is that someone close to him, such as a parent, would have to be identified as aggressive if he admitted that anyone was aggressive. To construe the parent as aggressive may have such far-reaching consequences that the better elaborative choice would seem to be to include the parent with the gentle ones, even if it means universalizing "gentleness." Any other interpretation on his part might shake the whole construction system which gives shape to his life role.

Often a speaker, by his choice of constructs, indicates what he thinks of the listener. This happens continually in psychotherapy; the psychotherapist gets a pretty good notion of what the client thinks of him by what the client chooses to emphasize or even to talk about. For example, the client who says, "Everyone is gentle," may be implying that the therapist is too prone to see aggressiveness. What he means is, "You seem to keep looking for aggressiveness; please take the view, when dealing with me, that everyone is gentle." Another similar interpretation is that he means, "Look, I'm such a nice person that I am willing to call everybody gentle, whether they are or not. Now don't you think I'm saintly?" Or he may mean, "So many people see aggressiveness around them and I am so upset by it that I try to exemplify the virtue of seeing gentleness."

Another possible interpretation is that the client is trying to express movement. Whereas once he saw the world as aggressive, he now sees it as gentle. Or he may be warning the therapist of impending movement: "So many people see the world as aggressive. I don't yet — but watch out!"

d. *Special problems of interpretation.* Since constructs are primarily personal, not all of them are easily shared. The peculiar nature of a person's construct or his unusual use of terminology may be misleading to his listener. For example, what one person means by "gentle" may correspond more closely to what others would call "dependent" or, perhaps, "weak." He may even have in mind some kind of refinement of manners, social status, or cultural grouping such as one might imply when he uses the term "gentleman."

Then one needs to be aware of the two-ended nature of the construct and the possibility that one person's "gentle" may have quite a different continuum stretching away from it than does another person's "gentle." We have suggested that the speaker might be construing in terms of a *gentle vs. aggressive* continuum. But perhaps the contrast end of his construct is not "aggressive" but something like "tactless" or, perhaps, "ingenuous." In that case, his statement might mean something more like, "Everyone is subtle," or, "Everyone is sly."

Sometimes a client is simply performing an experiment with his therapeutic role. He acts out a point of view in order to see how the therapist will respond or what the resulting situation will yield for him. He may mean, "Let's see how you react to this statement: 'Everyone is gentle.'" The key to understanding this kind of statement is to note the implied quotation marks in what the client says. The client is experimenting. If the therapist appears either to accept or reject the statement, the client interprets it as throwing light upon the therapist. If, for example, the therapist appears to accept the statement, it may mean that he is ill-prepared to deal with the latent aggression which the client might be hoping to express. If the therapist appears to reject the statement, it will next be important to find out what he considers aggression to be and who the aggressive people are. Perhaps the therapist, in that case, is getting ready to be aggressive himself.

Sometimes the client makes his statements in reverse form.

Like the experimental psychologist who, if he is precise, designs his experiments around the null hypothesis, which he really hopes will be rejected, the client may make tentative reverse bets. Instead of saying, "Is *not* the whole world aggressive?" he says, "The whole world is gentle." He uses an affirmative antithetical statement instead of the *not*. Having laid down the hypothesis, he proceeds to see how many holes the data of his experience will shoot into it. Perhaps the client is experimenting with himself. He may mean, "While I do not think so, I shall now pretend that the whole world is gentle; I wonder what preposterous things will happen *to me* in consequence of my taking this pose." Persons frequently experiment in these ways, a fact which the therapist needs to keep in mind continually. It is also a fact for which conventional learning theory in psychology has no facile explanation.

It is not our intention to make an exhaustive analysis of what a person means when he makes a simple declarative statement. It is sufficient to make clear that the contrast aspects of an expressed personal construct must not be overlooked in interpretation, and to point out that there is a great variety of possible interpretations that a listener may place upon such a simple statement as we have used for our illustration.

3. IMPLIED LINKAGES IN THE INTERPRETATION OF PERSONAL CONSTRUCTS

In the practical interpretation of personal constructs we need to be alerted to another feature of the way people express themselves. Let us take our original illustrative statement, "Mary and Alice have gentle dispositions but neither of them is as attractive as Jane." While it may appear that the speaker is invoking two different constructs in order to avoid mentioning the contrast end of one of them, he may have actually contraposed the ideas so that his construct functions as a *gentle vs. attractive* continuum. Gentleness and unattractiveness may be undifferentiated from each other in the speaker's construction system; also attractiveness and ungentleness. It may be that they have never been differentiated; or it may be that recent experience has, through construction, linked them, so that they now function as a single personal construct.

This kind of linkage is a common problem in psychotherapy. It is found in stereotypes and in the global *figure transferences* through which clients see their therapists and others during certain stages of treatment. This kind of linkage is sometimes interpreted by the therapist, in whose own system the terms seem clearly to refer to separate constructs, as "conflict." He does this because he has not yet entered into the client's thinking perceptively enough to see the singularity of the construct as it is used personally by the client. The "conflict" may be more the experience of the therapist than of the client. What the client experiences, assuming that the construct fails to work for him, is *anxiety*. But more about anxiety later!

The statement about Mary, Alice, and Jane may imply another kind of linkage, which stems from the person's own identification of himself with the context of the construct he uses. "Mary and Alice have gentle dispositions *but* neither of them is as attractive as Jane." The speaker may be using the two different constructs of *gentleness* and *attractiveness*. If he says simply that Mary and Alice are not as attractive as Jane, he will have identified himself as a detractor of Mary and Alice; so he first identifies himself as maintaining a pleasant relationship with Mary and Alice. Our social discourse is full of the *yes, but* . . . types of construction. They represent our efforts to be objective, not by keeping ourselves detached from the context of our discussion, but by allying ourselves with all parties in the context. "John is a nice fellow," "Jim is a swell guy," "Some of my best friends are Jews," are common prefaces designed to give immunity to the speaker against the consequences of what he is about to say.

Finally, there is the possibility of a kind of linkage which stems from the speaker's attempt to set up a *system* of constructs. The construct of *gentleness* is seen as subsuming the construct of *attractiveness*. Mary and Alice, by virtue of being gentle, are attractive. Jane is also attractive, but not because she is gentle.

We have pointed out the minimum context of three things out of which a construct can be formed, and the minimum of two relationships, one of likeness and one of difference, which must be implied. We have offered some introductory interpretations of the conceptual breakdown which may be implied in a speaker's simple statement; and, finally, we have suggested the linkage of constructs. One should not infer from this discussion that it is possible for a clinician, even though highly skilled, to assure himself that his client's conceptual system is breaking down in some area, merely from listening to one simple sentence of the type used in the illustration. As we have tried to illustrate, there are several possible interpretations of the personal constructs implied by the illustrative sentence. The alternatives are not so vast as to be unmanageable, however, and the skilled clinician may be able to tease out the meanings and linkages of the client's personal constructs, as expressed in such a sentence, without too great difficulty.

When conceptual distortion is detected, through noting the client's inability to accept at least a threefold context or a twofold relationship in expressing his construct, we have seen that the clinician may want to pay particular attention to the missing *opposites* implied by the construct, the implied momentary *role* in which the construct would force the speaker to cast himself in relation to the listener, the kind of *world* or cast of characters in relation to which he must establish a life role, the kind of experimental *venture* he may be attempting, and the kinds of subsuming relationships, or *system,* in which the client's constructs are ordered. With these points in mind, we can now turn our attention to some further basic implications of the psychology of personal constructs.

4. CONSTRUCTS AND ANTICIPATIONS

From what we have said thus far about the nature of constructs one might easily conclude that they are designed to set in order a universe composed of inherently static objects. Yet our Fundamental Postulate envisions a universe of processes. Indeed, it may seem as though we have inadvertently exposed our *construct* to the same modern criticism that is leveled at the Aristotelian *concept* — that it fails to deal with antecedence and subsequence. It is time, therefore, for us to take up more explicitly the part that construing plays in an anticipatory system of psychology.

We have said that a person's processes are psychologically channelized by the ways in which he anticipates events, and that these ways exist in the form of constructs. A construct, in turn, is an abstraction. By that we mean it is a property attributed to several events, by means of which they can be differentiated into two homogeneous groups. The invention of such a property is the act of abstracting. To construe events is to use this convenient trick of abstracting them in order to make sense out of them. Each person goes at it in his own way, more or less, and that is where the title of this book, *The Psychology of Personal Constructs,* comes from.

Now what about prediction? We have said that events are set apart from each other by the construing of their replications. That is to say, we look at the undifferentiated stream of circumstance flowing past us, and we try to find something about it that repeats itself. Once we have abstracted that property, we have a basis for slicing off chunks of time and reality and holding them up for inspection one at a time. On the other hand, if we fail to find such a property, we are left swimming in a shoreless stream, where there are no beginnings and no endings to anything. Thus the first step in prediction is to get hold of a solid fistful of something to predict. And this is done by construing, as we have assumed in our Construction Corollary.

Setting off an event so that it can be predicted is one step; but the moment we take this step we commit ourselves even further. By the very process of identifying the event as something replicated, we imply that it may happen again. Or, rather, we imply that its replicated properties may all reappear in another event. Thus it is impossible not to imply prediction whenever one construes anything. Certainly there is nothing static about a world which is construed in this manner.

a. *What is it that is predicted when one predicts?* When one abstracts replicated properties in the events he has already experienced, it becomes possible for him to chart events to come in terms of these same properties. A navigator who has never been to the North Pole may yet know its coordinates so well that he can predict the event of his arrival there. In a sense he does not conjure up the event itself, but rather its properties. Sure enough, twenty-nine days after he makes his prediction he does experience an event having all the predicted properties — time, declination of the sun, and so on — all occurring in conjunction with each other. With this evidence of the converging properties of time and space, he shouts to his companions, "Here we are; this is it!" His prediction is satisfactorily confirmed.

Let us make sure that we are explicit about this. What one predicts is not a fully fleshed-out event, but simply the common intersect of a certain set of properties. If an event comes along in which all the properties intersect in the prescribed way, one identifies it as the event he expected. For example, a girl in her teens anticipates eventual marriage. There are few men in her life and the system of constructs which she uses to keep them arranged is fairly simple. The predicted husband does not exist for her in the flesh, but simply as the intersect of a limited number of conceptual dimensions. One day a young man comes along and plumps himself down more or less on this waiting intersect. Her prediction, like the navigator's, is confirmed and, before anyone realizes what is happening, she marries him.

But take the old maid. She, too, has predicted a husband in terms of the intersect of a number of conceptual dimensions. But there are altogether too many dimensions involved and nobody ever lands on the precise point where all of them converge. Her long-standing anticipation is never fulfilled; she continues to be a spinster.

b. *Concretizing constructs.* We have taken some pains to point out that to understand whole events we have to abstract them. Now let us point out, in turn, that to understand constructs we have to concretize them. Thus to make sense out of concrete events we thread them through with constructs, and to make sense out of the constructs we must point them at events.

Here we have a full cycle of sense-making, the first phase of which is embedded in the traditions of rationalism, but the second phase of which conforms to the basic tenet of modern scientific experimentalism. Any theory, such as our theory of personality, must make good through both phases of the cycle. Not only must it give us a rationale of the events of human behavior, but it must result in predictions having their counterparts in tomorrow's reality.

The prediction in terms of which constructs are concretized is itself entirely hypothetical. It is the imagined intersect of several construct dimensions. Once it is made, it can be validated only if an event comes along which can be construed like the intersect. This is the experimental evidence one usually looks for. Through the accumulation of such evidence a theory gradually gets its feet on the ground.

c. *If-then relationships.* Let us turn from the structure of a prediction and look next at the process of arriving at it. This, too, is a construing process which starts with an abstraction. But a special kind of abstraction is involved. The construct one forms is a construct of trend or movement perceived amid the context of elements. As in the case of all constructs, the possibilities are twofold; the tendency can be in one direction or the other. The two poles of the construct establish the line along which the movement may take place.

Consider again our illustration of the navigator. Ever since he left his point of departure he has been observing various events. He has made records of chronometer readings, of the declinations of astral bodies, of magnetic and gyroscopic compass readings, and of track. To these events he applies constructs from his professional repertory. For example, he may apply the constructs of longitude and latitude. Next, in relation to these navigator's coordinates, he creates a special construct of movement, tailor-made to the situation. The construct will be dichotomous, of course; one pole refers to the direction in which he is going and the other to the direction he is coming from. With this construct in hand, together with the coordinates of the hypothetical North Pole and certain other constructs, he arrives at a prediction that twenty-nine days hence he will reach the Pole.

To predict is to construe movement or trend among surrounding events. The particular movement construed is always a construct tailor-made for a particular situation; nevertheless, it is one based on a standing system of coordinate axes having more general applicability. The point of convergence of all relevant constructs — time, the movement construct, and the coordinate readings of the hypothetical event — constitute the prediction. The next step is to see whether any event falls smack on this imaginary point so as to fulfill all of its presupposed conditions. That is validation.

Consider another illustration. A child predicts that if he breaks his mother's necklace he will get a spanking. He seems to perceive an *if-then* relationship between the breakage and the spanking. But this is never a simple one-to-one relationship, even to a child. To predict the spanking it is necessary for him to construe a considerable variety of events: his mother's disposition and mood, the value she places on the necklace, his own part in the breakage, the discovery of his act, a previous spanking or two, and the circumstances which surrounded the previous spankings. From these he abstracts a trend. At one pole of his trend construct are those events which lead away from a spanking; at the other are those which lead toward it. The events now confronting him look like those which lead toward the spanking. The child's construction does not have the mathematical qualities of the navigator's, but the process is basically identical.

d. *The contrasts implied in prediction.* Since a prediction is based on bipolar constructs, it tends to have an *if-then-but-not* quality. To have solid meaning the prediction must make a clean distinction between what will occur and what will not occur. This is what we mean by *differential* prediction. The child in our illustration predicted that he would get a spanking. But, in doing so, he also ruled out the opposite trend as a likelihood in his case; he predicted that he would *not* get a nod of approval from his mother.

To say that one thing will happen is also always to say that certain other things will not happen. Otherwise, our predictions would not be discriminating. A prediction always involves a negative forecast as well as a positive expectation. The range of convenience of the particular predictive system the person employs determines how extensively he implies, by his prediction, that certain things will not occur. Often in clinical work the therapist overlooks the specific negative implications of his clients' forecasts. When he does he is likely to be unduly surprised and confused by the clients' reactions to what appear to be extraneous events.

e. *Deductive use of constructs.* There is an if-then relationship implied in deduction. Since a construct is a two-ended thing, one would, in using our illustration of Mary, Alice, and Jane, say, "*If* this person is gentle, *then* she could be Mary or Alice or —— *but not* Jane or ——." Under our view of constructs the structure becomes an if-then-but-not form of reasoning. The elements which follow the *then* are the *like* elements in the context and the elements which follow the *not* are the *contrast* elements in the context. Elements outside the context are not touched by the construct, nor are they involved in the prediction. If Mary, Alice, and Jane constituted the entire context of the construct — that is, if the construct did not cover any other persons in its context — then our statement would become simply, "If this person is gentle, she is Mary or Alice, and she is definitely not Jane." She could even be both, if those were her two names. She may or may not be Elizabeth, Ann, or Joan — those might be her other names also. But of this much we are sure, if she is *gentle,* and the complete context of *gentle* is Mary-like-Alice-in-contrast-to-Jane, then she is Mary or Alice, but not Jane.

The construct may be employed inductively, although, as everyone who has tried to draw generalizations from research knows, this involves practical difficulties. In this case the form is slightly changed. We may say, "*If* this person is Mary or Alice *but not* Jane, *then* this person is gentle." This is an if-but-not-then form of reasoning.

Suppose the context of *gentle* is limited to Mary, Alice, and Jane. Then we must come to the somewhat startling conclusion that any contextual arrangement of these three figures, and these three figures only, in which Mary and Alice are linked in contrast to Jane, is, in fact, the construct of *gentle*. There would be no basis for the existence of any other construct — that is, any other construct would thus be identical with *gentle*. If, however, on one occasion Mary and Alice were linked in contrast to Jane, and on another Mary, Alice, and Elizabeth were linked in contrast to Jane, then there would be operational grounds for distinguishing two different constructs.

Our if-then-but-not relationship takes on an interesting connotation when we see such a term as "Mary" as itself the symbol of abstraction. This involves the notion of superordination. Suppose a series of events is construed in terms of its Mary-ness. Indeed, that is what a person really is — an abstraction of a series of events. Let us suppose that *Mary-ness* is further abstracted as *gentle*. Then we may, as we have in our illustration of the deductive use of a construct, use our if-then-but-not form. *If* this is Mary-ness, *then* gentle things *but not* aggressive things are to be expected.

Sometimes, as all of us know, even such a paragon of gentleness as Mary has turned out to be in our series of illustrations fails to act in a gentle manner. Actually Mary is abstracted at several levels. In her more material abstraction she is sometimes known to act in an ungentle manner. We say then that she is revealing the "human side of her nature." Or we may say, "Mary is not herself today." Or we may say, "This is not the Mary I was referring to." What we mean is that the Mary-ness that we construe as gentle is not a feature of today's events; what we have today is a lower order of Mary-ness, a person abstracted in a somewhat different manner.

5. CONSTRUCTS AS CONTROLS

Constructs are the channels in which one's mental processes run. They are two-way streets along which one may travel to reach conclusions. They make it possible to anticipate the changing tides of events. For the reader who is more comfortable with teleological terms it may be helpful to say that constructs are the controls that one places upon life — the life within him as well as the life which is external to him. Forming constructs may be considered as binding sets of events into convenient bundles which are handy for the person who has to lug them. Events, when so bound, tend to become predictable, manageable, and controlled.

Let us recall what we said about determinism and free will. We described them as essentially complementary aspects of the same hierarchical structure. That which is subsumed by a construct may be seen as determined by it; that which subsumes the construct is free with respect to it. Now we may approach *control* as a special case of the aspect of determinism. If we explain the goings on in nature in terms of theological constructs, it is God who determines everything that happens and it is He who controls our destiny. If, for the moment, we take a series of more constricted views, we may see the control vested in geophysical processes, or in social forces, or in the national economy, or in local business conditions, or in the administration of our university, or in the orneriness of a certain man. Control, like determinism, is not an absolutistic construct; it depends on which way one is looking. If he looks up the street, he sees control; if he looks down the same street, he sees spontaneity.

But does a man control his own destiny? Our answer to that is that he may control it to the extent that he can develop a construction system with which he identifies himself and which is sufficiently comprehensive to subsume the world around him. If he is unable to identify himself with the system, he may be able to predict events determinatively, but he can experience no personal control. If he is able to develop the system as a self-system as well as a not-self-system, and can make it work — in other words, predict — he may exercise control. According to this view, mankind is slowly learning to control his destiny, although it is a long and tedious process. Furthermore, this view, since it is framed within the position of constructive alternativism, does not necessarily negate the view of man as the result of social forces or of man as the servant of a supreme being.

It is no accident that the intellect has been classically described as the controlling feature of the human mind. The intellect has been associated with communicable constructs. When a person communicates the construct under which he is operating, we too can see what he is doing. His behavior then makes sense to us; we understand him. When he fails to communicate his construct, his behavior is likely not to make sense, and we say that he is stupid and his behavior is uncontrolled. Usually we can see more clearly the patterns into which another person's behavior falls in those instances in which he is able to convey to us a clear understanding of the personal constructions which are governing it. It is not surprising, therefore, that we are inclined to assume that it is the communicable or intellectualized constructs which provide the neatest controls upon people's behavior.

The term "control" is frequently used in describing patients. Sometimes psychologists speak of "overcontrol." But to our way of thinking, control, in general, is a point of view from which we seek to explain any behavior. To say that something is out of control is merely to say that we have given up trying to explain it. To abandon the notion of control, with respect to any behavior whatsoever, is to abandon the notion of lawfulness.

Now what about "intellectual control" or "overintellectualized control" in the patient? The person who continually expresses, in some communicable form, the constructs under which he sees himself operating is likely to be described in a clinic as "overintellectualized." If he were less articulate, the clinician would probably not give him that label. Also, he would probably avoid the label if he expressed his constructs less clearly. Furthermore, and this is probably important in psychotherapy, if he had not shared his constructs with so many other people or with people with whom he is presently so closely identified, he might be able to reshuffle them without altering his basic role relationships.

One way to think of the construct is as a pathway of movement. The two-ended construct provides a person with a dichotomous choice, whether it be a choice in how he will perceive something or a choice in how he will act. One may say, therefore, that the system of constructs which one establishes for himself represents the network of pathways along which he is free to move. Each pathway is a two-way street; he can move either up or down the street, but he cannot strike out across country without building new conceptual routes to follow. Whether he goes up or down a particular street is a matter of choice, and we have indicated that this choice is governed by what we call the principle of the elaborative choice.

The network of pathways which is formed by the construction system may be considered as a system of controls, but each one represents an opportunity for a dichotomous choice. The choice, in turn, is controlled by the principle of the elaborative choice. Thus, as we have already indicated, the deterministic and the free features of one's psychological system exist together. Since the construct does not pretend to say which of its two ends shall be chosen, it leaves the person free to choose; since it does say what its two ends are, it controls the possibilities of choice. The principle of the elaborative choice, on the other hand, does control the choice that is made within a construct dimension, but it leaves the person free to decide what it is that will give him the greater opportunity for further definition and elaboration of his system.

When a person must move he is confronted with a series of dichotomous choices. Each choice is channelized by a construct. As he reconstrues himself he may either rattle around in his old slots or he may construct new pathways across areas which were not previously accessible. When he is under pressure he is not likely to develop new channels; instead he will tend to reverse himself along the dimensional lines which have already been established. If he is a client, and his therapist merely exhorts him to change himself, this will be the type of movement open to him. If the emergency is great and the pressure is intense, the movement is likely to be abortive. In that case he will show marked contrast behavior along the major axes of his personality. If the therapist is willing to approach the treatment more circumspectly, it is often possible to develop some new channels within which the client can work out his readjustment. In that case the movement is often less drastic but more appropriate. But whether a client develops new constructs to channelize his movement, or whether he rattles around in the old slots, the constructs of his system may be considered both as controls and as pathways along which he is free to move.

Dewey emphasized the anticipatory nature of behavior and the person's use of hypotheses in thinking. The psychology of personal constructs follows Dewey in this respect. From our position each construct represents a pair of rival hypotheses, either of which may be applied to a new element which the person seeks to construe. This thing that I hold in my hand: is it black or is it white? Black and white are the rival hypotheses which are set up by the *black vs. white* construct. Thus, just as the experimental scientist designs his experiments around rival hypotheses, so each person designs his daily explorations of life around the rival hypotheses which are suggested by the contrasts in his construction system. Moreover, just as the scientist cannot foresee possibilities that he has not somehow conceptualized in terms of hypotheses, so any individual can prove or disprove only that which his construction system tells him are the possible alternatives. Again the construction system sets the limits beyond which it is impossible for him to perceive. His constructs are controls on his outlook.

There are many ramifications to this issue of control and they are particularly interesting, it seems to us, in the area of psychotherapy. Our main point, at this juncture in our exposition of the psychology of personal constructs, is that constructs are pathways of freedom of movement. Because they are two-way channels they provide freedom for the person who possesses them; because he can move only along these pathways they represent restrictive controls upon everything that he does. Moreover, our view of constructs does not limit them to those which are symbolized by words, or even to those which can be communicated by means of pantomime. Perhaps the psychology of personal constructs is an intellectualized theory. But if, by intellectual controls, one means that the constructs are communicated, then there are some kinds of controls which are not intellectual, since they are not communicated. A large portion of human behavior follows nameless channels which have no language symbols, nor any kinds of signposts whatsoever. Yet they are channels and they are included in the network of dichotomous dimensions with relation to which the person's world is structured.

The psychology of personal constructs is built upon an intellectual model, to be sure, but its application is not intended to be limited to that which is ordinarily called intellectual or cognitive. It is also taken to apply to that which is commonly called emotional or affective and to that which has to do with action or conation. The classical threefold division of psychology into cognition, affection, and conation has been completely abandoned in the psychology of personal constructs.

While the psychology of personal constructs is concerned with personal constructs all of which may not be communicable, and hence is not really what some would call intellectualized theory, it is important that it be itself communicated and that it be intellectually comprehensible. Here we distinguish between the personal constructs about which the theory is concerned and the constructs which constitute the approach of the theory itself. The former may or may not be communicated; the latter must be communicated to make public sense. If the psychology of personal constructs turns out to be no more than the fulminations of the writer rattling around in his own personal construct slots, it will scarcely be worth committing to print. The understanding of this manuscript will be one of the practical tests of whether or not the psychology of personal constructs can be communicated.

6. THE PERSONAL CONSTRUCTION OF ONE'S ROLE

Let us turn our attention, more particularly, to the controlling effect one's constructs have upon himself. As we have pointed out before, the *self* is, when considered in the appropriate context, a proper concept or construct. It refers to a group of events which are alike in a certain way and, in that same way, necessarily different from other events. The way in which the events are alike is the self. That also makes the self an individual, differentiated from other individuals. The self, having been thus conceptualized, can now be used as a thing, a datum, or an item in the context of a superordinate construct. The self can become one of the three or more things — or persons — at least two of which are alike and are different from at least one of the others.

When the person begins to use himself as a datum in forming constructs, exciting things begin to happen. He finds that the constructs he forms operate as rigorous controls upon his behavior. His behavior in relation to other people is particularly affected. Perhaps it would be better to say that his behavior *in comparison* with other people is particularly affected. It is, of course, the comparison *he* sees or construes which affects his behavior. Thus, much of his social life is controlled by the comparisons he has come to see between himself and others.

We have already discussed the distortion of conceptualization that occurs when one is reluctant to express the full context or relationships of his construct and how, in some instances, the full expression of the construct would commit the speaker to a role which he does not want to play. For example, the statement, "Mary, Alice, Jane, and everyone else are always gentle," may indicate that the distortion is at the point at which the person is on the verge of casting himself in the role of one who must deal with ungentle people. If the only counterpoise against aggression is aggression, and if aggression, in turn, is linked tightly in a personal chain of constructs which would inferentially deny the person his identifying role, he is likely to avoid saying that anyone is "not gentle." In very simple and tentative language, one does not ask to be seen in a role he cannot handle and he does not elaborate the role he is not ready to play.

The personal construction of one's role may also be inferred, as we shall see later in connection with a discussion of the Role Construct Repertory Test, from the construction he places upon other people. One of the clinical uses of Murray's Thematic Apperception Test is to make an analysis of the human figures portrayed as well as an analysis of the themes or story plots. Indeed, most clinicians tend to emphasize the figure type of analysis to the exclusion of the thematic type of analysis. From the figure analysis one is able to get some idea of what kind of people populate the client's world. By understanding the cast of the play, and, from a thematic analysis, by understanding the plot of the play, the examiner may infer the kind of role the examinee must see cut out for himself. Sometimes that role is even described explicitly by the examinee as he attributes ideas and actions to the principal actor in the story he makes up.

But this is not the only way in which the examinee's response to the test reveals his casting of himself; it is revealed in the constructs in terms of which he describes the people he reads into the pictures or weaves into his plot. Each construct has its contrast features. The clinician who administers the test needs to take account of the contrasts which are implied by the examinee's descriptions of the persons in the pictures. These contrast features also play a part in the examinee's construction of his role. This is a point which can easily be overlooked in the interpretation of Thematic Apperception Test performance.

When, in an intake interview, a client describes the other people who populate his intimate world, he is essentially stating the coordinate axes with reference to which he must plot his own behavior. He is stating his personal construct system. Too often the clinician does not realize what a rich source of potentially useful information about the client is being revealed. He may garble the interpretation of the interview by trying to find out whether or not Aunt Olga was really as mean an old buzzard as the client is describing her. Or worse still, he may simply identify the client's statement about Aunt Olga as a cold fact which is not subject to later reinterpretation by the client. The really important thing about the client's statement of Aunt Olga's sins may be that he is describing a role to which he is, at times, partially committed himself, or a role to which, even now, he must play an opposite or complementary part.

As one construes other people, he formulates the construction system which governs his own behavior. The constructs which have other people as their contexts bind oneself too. One cannot call another person a bastard without making bastardy a dimension of his own life also.

But, again, let us remind ourselves that a construct is a *single* formulation of a likeness *and* a difference. To call another person a bastard is not necessarily to conceptualize oneself as a bastard. One may conceptualize himself as definitely *not* being a bastard. The important point for the clinician to understand is that the client has ordered his world with respect to the dimension of bastardy.

A construct is a two-ended thing, not merely a category of likeness with no inferred difference in the offing. One cannot refer to the likeness aspect of the construct without simultaneously invoking the difference aspect of the construct. Many years ago Freud pointed out that in dreams ideas were frequently represented by their opposites. Since dreams also deal in constructs, it is not so surprising that in them the constructs sometimes remain intact but are merely turned end for end. The clinician who regularly applies the psychology of personal constructs should not be misled by this simple upending of a construct.

Now something very interesting happens when a person first seeks to readjust to life with the framework of his personal system of constructs. The dimensions, of course, tend to remain the same. His freedom of movement, therefore, at first appears to him to be possible only along the axes which he has already established for himself. Let us suppose, for example, that he has oriented his role with respect to the personal construct of *gentleness vs. aggressiveness.* Let us suppose he has classified himself as like the gentle people in his construct context. He is one of the gentle ones. Next, suppose the act starts to misfire. He misses his cues, bobbles his lines. Something has gone wrong with his anticipation system. There are too many rude surprises. It becomes apparent that he must do something about his role. The most obvious thing to do is to start reclassifying his role within the contexts of some of his personal role constructs. Suppose he decides to move it along the *gentleness-aggressiveness* axis. He does so. A few weeks later his friends remark, "What's happened to Casper? My, my, how he has changed!"

The chances are that Casper has not really changed his adjustment system but has tried to reassociate himself within whatever limited construction system he had to work with. A study of so-called marked personality changes, such as the manic-depressive cycle, confirms the fact that most of the radical movements that we see appearing in people's behavior do not represent basic changes in their blueprints of life, but rather an attempt to shift within the rigid frameworks which provide their only cues to the understanding of human relationships. If a clinician is aware of a client's dimensional system, he can make some prediction of the *directions* in which the client would have to move if he were required to jump quickly.

A psychotherapist who seeks to force his client to move too rapidly runs into just this type of problem. He forces the client to move along the only axes the client has previously established for himself and the results may be catastrophic. Even if the psychotherapist proceeds slowly, yet is not aware of what the personal construct system is, he may find his client moving in totally unexpected directions.

While one's personal constructs represent the controlling system in which one's role is played out or readjusted, it is possible, under favorable conditions, for the person to readjust the constructs himself. To use the mathematical expression, he can rotate the axes on life. This will give him a new set of dimensions and new obvious directions of freedom of movement.

A person's reconstruction of life is a process which goes on all the time. Actually it is impossible for a person to reverse his stance with respect to one of his role-governing constructs without changing the construct in some measure. In psychotherapy a concerted effort is frequently made to help the person formulate new and rather basic constructs with respect to which his conception of role may be reoriented. It is almost essential that these new basic constructs first be formulated in contexts that do not involve the client too intimately before such a fundamental system as that which governs his own role is challenged. The client who is suddenly told that he must change himself is likely to be seriously threatened, and may either become inaccessible to treatment or be panicked into making violent evasive movements within his old framework.

If the new constructs are first developed in contexts which do not involve the client or members of his immediate and present family, the paralyzing threat of premature movement may be avoided. Very soon, however, the person himself must be involved in the new construct formation. If it is avoidable, his whole self should not be committed to the construct's context all at once. One approach is to commit only the client's past self to the context; let him re-sort himself as he was when he was a child. Another way is to sort out certain behaviors only, say those which can be observed wholly within the confines of the treatment room. Another way is to construct artificial roles and play them out.

But more of this later. The principal points are that construct systems control the role one plays in life, that they are revealed by the client whenever he talks about other people, as well as when he talks about himself, that the constructs which control one's role are two-ended or dimensional in character, that the most obvious freedom of movement that one can see is from one end to the other along the axes he has already personally construed for himself, and that the construct systems that control one's role can, under favorable circumstances, be changed.

7. THE REAL NATURE OF CONSTRUCTS

We have long since committed ourselves to a point of view from which we see the world as being real and man's psychological processes as being based upon personal versions of that reality. The personal versions are personal constructs. Now we may ask ourselves the question whether, from this point of view, constructs are real. The answer is a qualified yes. Constructs are not to be confounded with the factual material of which they are personalized versions; they are interpretations of those facts. But constructs may be used as viewpoints for seeing other constructs, as in the hierarchical relationships of constructs within a system. In that sense the superordinate constructs are versions of those constructs which are subordinate to them. This makes the subordinate constructs a form of reality which is construed through the use of the superordinate constructs. The summary answer to our question of whether or not constructs are real is that a construct is indeed real, but its reality is not identical with the factual elements in its context. With respect to the factual elements it is representative, not identical. Its reality is not their reality. The construct has its own reality. The problem should not cause us trouble if we keep in mind that a construct and its elements are both real, but distinguished from each other.

Can a construct be communicated from one person to another without losing its reality? In a sense the answer is yes. It is not, of course, transferred from one person to another like the one eye of the three Graeae in Greek mythology: when one got it the other two lost it. The notion of communication is itself a construct and, just as we let a construct represent that of which it is a construction, we let a communicated construct represent the personal construct of which it is a construction. The communicated construct is the construing of the person who "receives" it; one of its elements is the construct of the person who had it beforehand. The construct of the person from whom the communication takes place is real; so is the communicated construct, but the communicated construct is a construction of the original construct and hence not identical with it. In this sense the answer to our question about whether or not a construct can be communicated from one person to another without losing its reality is definitely yes. A construct does not change its allegiance when someone else gets a version of it.

B. Formal Aspects of Constructs

8. TERMINOLOGY

a. *Range of convenience.* We have already indicated that a theory or system has a range within which it serves the user conveniently for the job of predicting events. We have also indicated in our assumptive structure for the psychology of personal constructs that a construct has a range of convenience. The range of convenience of a construct would cover all those things to which the user found its application useful.

b. *Focus of convenience.* A construct may be maximally useful for handling certain matters. The range of these matters is called its focus of convenience.

c. *Elements.* The things or events which are abstracted by a construct are called elements.

d. *Context.* The context of a construct is composed of all those elements to which the construct is ordinarily applied. It is somewhat more constricted than the range of convenience, since it refers to the circumstances in which the construct emerges and not necessarily to all the circumstances in which a person might eventually use the construct. It is somewhat more extensive than the focus of convenience, since the construct may often emerge in circumstances in which its application is not altogether optimal.

e. *Pole.* Each construct involves two poles, one at each end of its dichotomy. The elements associated at each pole are like each other with respect to the construct and are unlike the elements at the other pole.

f. *Contrast.* The relationship between the two poles of a construct is one of contrast.

g. *Likeness end.* When referring specifically to elements at one pole of a construct we have used the term *likeness end,* meaning that we are referring to the pole at which these elements are grouped by the construction.

h. *Contrast end.* When referring specifically to elements at the opposite pole of a construct, we have used the term *contrast end,* meaning that we are referring to the other pole.

i. *Emergence.* Here we borrow Lyle's construct. The emergent pole of a construct is that which embraces most of the immediately perceived context. For example, in the statement, "Mary and Alice are gentle but Jane is aggressive," gentleness is emergent because it refers to two thirds of the context. Frequently only the emergent pole is explicitly mentioned, as when a person says, "Mary and Alice are gentle but Jane is not."

j. *Implicitness.* Again we borrow from Lyle's thinking. The implicit pole of a construct is the one which contrasts with the emergent pole. It is frequently not mentioned by name. Sometimes the person has no symbolization for it; it is symbolized only implicitly by the emergent term.

9. SYMBOLISM

Any one of the like elements in the context of one's construct may give the construct its name. A construct, formed in the context of A, B, and C, with A and B being the *like* elements, may be represented simply by the mentioning of A. Now A may itself, in turn, be a true construct, originating in a context of A_a, A_b, and A_c; we are not referring to A's use in this sense but rather to its use as a representative for or as a symbol of the construct formed out of a context comprising A, B, and C. A may then be used to represent a construct which is not A at all but really one which subsumes A, a higher-order construct which really has A as a part of its context only. This is the basic nature of symbolism.

Symbolism is a handy tool. Understood in the light of the above paragraph, it is not the sole tool for shaping thought but is certainly a very useful and commonly used one.

Man has developed a neat trick in the use of symbolism. He makes up sounds and shapes and introduces them artificially into the context of his constructs as one of the elements. Then he lets this sound or shape become a symbol of the construct. For example, he adds the word "gentleness" to Mary and Alice so that now the context reads, "Mary, Alice, and gentleness versus Jane." From now on *gentleness* is used to represent the kinship of Mary, Alice, and the word "gentleness."

There is a simpler type of symbolism which does not involve the invasion of words into the context of a construct. We can let Mary become the symbol for gentleness and Jane the symbol for attractiveness. Mother can become the symbol for social belongingness. Father can become the symbol for maturity. In most people Mother and Father do represent personal constructs of a much higher order than their own identities necessitate. This kind of figure symbolism is characteristic of the personal constructs one forms in childhood. Moreover, these constructs are likely to be retained in terms of figure symbolism, an important fact for the psychotherapist. For a psychotherapist to say that a person "introjects" his father and mother is to miss the point; rather, his father and mother are likely to have been contextual elements in a great many of the personal constructs which the person has formed, particularly his role constructs. They may or may not be employed actually as symbols of these constructs.

We have said that figure symbolism is characteristic of the symbolism used to represent personal constructs formed in childhood. It is possible to state the case more generally. The use of one of the original contextual elements as the symbol of a construct is characteristic of the early stages in the formation and use of any construct. The construct of *Mary-like-Alice-unlike-Jane* is likely to be symbolized in the person's thinking simply as *Mary* or *Mary-ness*.

As new members are added to the context of the construct, assuming that it is a permeable construct, or as he seeks to invoke Mary-ness behavior in his friends, the person may contrive a verbal symbol. If the construct happens to be relatively impermeable or not communicated, except in the most intimate ways, it may continue to be represented symbolically simply by one of its original contextual elements. For example, if *mother* is the contextual element used to represent a certain personal construct which is relatively impermeable — for example, "Now there is no one like my mother" — or if no effort is made to communicate the personal construct — for example, "No one could possibly understand what my mother was really like" — then "my mother" is likely to be retained as the symbol as well as one of the contextual elements of the personal construct.

Through most of this discussion of personal constructs we have been using people or "figures" to illustrate the contextual elements of personal constructs. It is believed that such constructs are of paramount importance to the psychologist. But what we have said is also true of personal constructs about other things. The construct of *speed* may be symbolized by an automobile as well as by a word. The construct of *comfort* may be symbolized by a curve like that of the mother's breast; the construct of *rectitude* may be symbolized by the sound of a firm, masculine voice; or the construct of *virility* may be symbolized by an erect penis. The "blood and guts" type of response on the Rorschach Test may, in certain instances, be a symbol of a personal construct lifted directly from the construct's context. In evaluating such a response it is essential for the clinician to find out (a) what the construct is and (b) what is its level of generality — that is, what order of elements it subsumes.

10. COMMUNICATION

Having portrayed symbolism in the above manner, we have also committed ourselves to a point of view regarding the nature of communication. If symbolism is a matter of letting one of the elements in the context of a construct appear as the representative of the construct itself, then communication is a matter of reproducing the symbolic element in hopes of eliciting a parallel construct in another person. The neatest way is to use a word as a symbol. Of course, it may not work, for our listener may not have incorporated the word into the same kind of context, or have used it as a symbol of the same construct. Then we may have to trot out other elements of our personal construct's context, some of them words, some of them nonverbal acts. With luck we may succeed in communicating, at least at an approximate level.

The client who attempts to communicate his personal constructs to a therapist can rarely depend upon simple verbal statements to communicate the precise personal nature of his constructs. He has to bring out for display a long list of other contextual elements before the therapist can understand. It is particularly difficult to communicate with a therapist if the personal construct is relatively impermeable and there are no contemporary elements which can readily be used to illustrate the context. It is difficult to communicate with the therapist if he does not appear to understand the subordinate constructs out of which the construct is formed. Finally, it is difficult to communicate with the therapist if the construct is a role-governing one which cannot be communicated without distorting the role relationship the client has established between himself and the therapist.

The therapist, on his side of the table, must not be too ready to impose his own preexisting personal constructs upon the symbolism and behavior of the client. He will first have to compile a lexicon for dealing with the client. Moreover, he will have to accept the possibility that the client's relations with him will vacillate markedly as the client illustrates, with naked realism, the contextual elements of his role-governing constructs.

11. SCALES OF CONSTRUCTS

From time to time we have used the notion of a construct as if it were an axis or a dimension. Since we have assumed that constructs are essentially dichotomous, it may appear that we have ruled out the possibility of scales or continua involving more than two steps. For example, Landfield, who performed interesting studies of threat from the standpoint of earlier formulations of personal-construct theory, had originally developed tailor-made scales of personal constructs for each of his subjects to use. He observed, however, that "'Dimensional scale' may be a misnomer, since it soon becomes apparent that many subjects who perceived people in degrees construed them, for example, not as a series of varying grays, but rather in terms of black, white and combinations of black and white." Even though we envision the basic constructs out of which our systems are built as dichotomous, it is still possible to conceive of gradations, as Landfield did, along a dimensional line.

There are several ways in which this kind of conception can be presented.

a. *Hierarchical scales.* Just as it is possible to express an infinite number of gradations of value in terms of binary number systems, so it is possible to express an infinite number of gradations of value in terms of a dichotomous construct system. One may construct such a scale by assuming a hierarchy of constructs. Consider a hierarchy of four constructs in the order of A, B, C, and D, each of which has two possible values, 0 and 1. A *hierarchical scale* of values may be built up from these four constructs. It will have $\log_2^{-1} 4$ or sixteen steps. The values of the sixteen steps can be represented by the first sixteen numbers of the binary system as follows:

$$
\begin{array}{c}
0000 \\
0001 \\
0010 \\
0011 \\
0100 \\
0101 \\
0110 \\
0111 \\
1000 \\
1001 \\
1010 \\
1011 \\
1100 \\
1101 \\
1110 \\
1111
\end{array}
$$

Suppose we build a hierarchical scale of *integrity vs. disintegrity* out of the four basic constructs of *honesty vs. dishonesty, candor vs. deviousness, courage vs. defeatism,* and *objectivity vs. subjectivity.* Suppose, also, that these constructs are arranged in that hierarchical order. Let the binary digit 1 represent the first of each pair and the binary digit 0 represent the second of each pair. A dishonest, devious, defeatist, subjective person would be represented by the scale value of 0000 and would be at the *disintegral* end of the scale. An honest but devious, defeatist, subjective person would be represented by the number 1000. Because of the high relevance of honesty to integrity, he rates in the upper half of the scale. A person who was dishonest, devious, defeatist, and objective would be represented by the number 0001 and would still be near the bottom of the scale.

b. *Additive scales.* Constructs can also be formed into an additive type of scale. Suppose we drop the notion of a hierarchy of constructs and simply add the binary digits representing the poles of the constructs. Now an honest but devious, defeatist, subjective person would score 1 for honesty and 0 for each of his other characteristics. His scale value would therefore be 0001. If he were also courageous instead of defeatist his score would be boosted to 0010. It is clear that this kind of scale would have only five steps instead of sixteen. The values would run from 0000 to 0100.

c. *Abstracted scales.* We can build another kind of scale by stepping up to a higher level of abstraction. Let us call it an *abstracted scale.* Suppose we construe *integrity vs. disintegrity*, not in terms of any concrete accumulation of the other four constructs, as we have in the two types of scale previously described, but as an abstraction of them. *Integrity vs. disintegrity* is now seen as a property which runs through the other four constructs. More particularly, it is a property of the relationship between any pairing of the constructs. For example, *honesty* in comparison with *dishonesty* is *integral* while *dishonesty* is *disintegral*, but mere *honesty* in comparison with *courage* might be considered *disintegral.* The construct of *integrity vs. disintegrity* is still dichotomous. Its abstraction, however, is relative, and in order to symbolize its application to shifting context one has to set up a whole row of symbols or numbers. This, of course, is a temptation to the user to employ the construct concretistically, and often that is precisely what happens.

We could depart from the central course of our discussion at this point and mention the difficulty many of us have in using a number system abstractly rather than concretely. For a child, a series of numbers is a concrete arrangement of named things.

As he grows older he finds that his number system can be used to arrange many different kinds of objects, but his numbers may still be concretistically perceived as mileage readings on a speedometer or weight readings on a scale. Still later, if he is lucky, he may be able to use his number system relativistically; when he abstracts the numerical value of *four* it is its *moreness* in relation to *three, two,* and *one,* and its *lessness* than *five, six,* and *seven* that he perceives.

d. *Approximation scales.* There is a fourth type of scale which is an artifact of people's trying to understand each other. Let us call this an *approximation scale.* Suppose an experimenter has a notion of *integrity vs. disintegrity* which is essentially dichotomous. He asks his subject to rate certain acquaintances on this scale. The subject, not being sure that what he would call "integrity" is the same as what the experimenter would call "integrity," tends to give compromise ratings. Only in those instances where the acquaintance appears to exhibit some combination of characteristics which seems clearly to be what the experimenter has in mind, will the subject venture to give an extreme rating. From this point of view, indeed from the point of view of the psychology of personal constructs, a leptokurtic distribution of scores on a scale is a clear indication of its approximate nature. The less the subject feels that he understands what the experimenter has in mind, the more he will hug some point on the scale, such as the middle, which seems to commit him the least. We can use this idea to infer how well a person understands the scale on which he is asked to make ratings. When the often mentioned J-curve or U-curve phenomena are observed, as in cases of cultural agreement, one may infer that the rater understands the prescribed construct well enough to make dichotomous ratings.

e. *Accumulation scales.* There is still another kind of scale which happens to be related to the additive scale. Let us call it an *accumulative scale.* Suppose two people have been observed on twenty different occasions. The first person has shown integral behavior nineteen out of twenty times while the second person has shown disintegral behavior nineteen out of twenty times.

Each person is given a score which represents approximately the proportion of occasions on which he has shown integral behavior. The construct of *integral vs. disintegral* remains essentially dichotomous; it is the accumulation of occasions which gives us an opportunity to assign more than two values to the degree of integrity.

f. *Other scales.* There are other ways in which scales built upon dichotomous constructs can be conceptualized. One could, for example, evaluate critical incidents and, disregarding the *number* of occasions in which he showed integrity, give a person a high score if he showed integrity in a *single* highly critical incident. Again a person could be rated on an integrity scale in terms of the proportion of his friends who classified him as integral. But it is not our intent to make an exhaustive analysis of the kinds of scales which people build; we wish only to make clear that the notion of dichotomous constructs does not preclude the use of scales. The notion does, however, lead one to look closely at all his scales and try to determine exactly what discriminative bases they may have.

12. SCANNING BY MEANS OF CONSTRUCTS

While we have not committed ourselves to following a cybernetic model in constructing the theory of personal constructs, our assumptions permit us to visualize certain psychological processes in terms of electronic analogues. When a person scans the events with which he is surrounded he "lights up" certain dichotomies in his construct system. Thus construct systems can be considered as a kind of scanning pattern which a person continually projects upon his world. As he sweeps back and forth across his perceptual field he picks up blips of meaning. The more adequate his scanning pattern, the more meaningful his world becomes. The more in tune it is with the scanning patterns used by others, the more blips of meaning he can pick up from their projections.

Viewed in this manner the psychology of personal constructs commits us to a projective view of all perception. All interpersonal relations are based essentially on transference relations, though they are subject to validation and revision. All test performances are best understood as projective test performances. In psychotherapy it becomes important to retune the client's scanning pattern. In learning and teaching it becomes important to know just what dichotomies in the pattern are being validated.

We may also think of constructs as providing ordinal axes in psychological space, the abscissas being provided by the temporal events themselves. With both constructs and events providing axes, the person builds a grid within whose quadrants his psychological space takes on multidimensional meaning. With respect to the ordinates there are many personal versions of what the axes are, but with respect to the abscissa of time we have a common experience. We may not agree with each other as to what the essential nature of an event is, but we can usually agree, subject to retrospective falsification, as to what the sequence is.

In a later chapter we shall indicate how the Repertory Grid can be used to lay out certain areas of a person's scanning pattern, how it can be factor analyzed by nonparametric methods, how certain problems of generalization of learning can be studied, and how the personal construct system can be related to public construct systems. It is sufficient for our purposes at this juncture simply to invite attention to the fact that the personal construct system can be viewed cybernetically.

13. PERSONAL SECURITY WITHIN THE CONTEXT OF A CONSTRUCT

We have mentioned the fact that the self may be used as one of the elements in the context of a construct (though we can imagine some constructs in which the self does not fall within the range of convenience). We have called attention to the governing effect of such a construct in the person's playing out his life role. In another section we pointed out the frequent use of figure symbolism, as contrasted with word symbolism, in the representation of a construct. For example, one's own mother might become the symbol of a certain role-fixing construct. Now let us consider what may ensue when various shifts in the elements of such a construct are attempted.

Suppose the elements on the like-mother side of a person's *mother* construct include, as they frequently do, a considerable variety of comforts, protections, and securities. As long as a person construes himself on the like-mother side of the construct, or on the like-mother-wants-me side of the construct, he may perceive himself as heir to these comforts, protections, and securities. But suppose the person's therapist attempts to shift the self from the like-mother side of the personal construct to the unlike-mother side. The unlike-mother context includes all of the relevant contrast features of the personal construct of *mother* — discomforts, hazards, and insecurities. What happens to the client?

Having come to see himself in this new global fashion, he may be expected to demonstrate new behaviors. He may abandon many of the constricted and cautious ways of comporting himself and start behaving in many ways that seem to him to be in contrast to the like-mother pole of his *mother* construct. He may become markedly adventuresome. His behavior may also become more diffuse as he plunges into new experiences and finds that he must face the unfamiliar events into which the new role precipitates him. This may prove to be an exhilarating experience, provided he has enough well-defined structure remaining to avoid the confusion of anxiety and if he has permeable constructs which adequately span both the old and the new behavior patterns. On the other hand, he may, through lack of structure to handle the new role, become markedly anxious.

If the client identifies himself with the unlike-mother side of his one mother-symbolized construct, he may, through the use of figure symbolism, find himself construed on the unlike-mother side of all mother-symbolized constructs. He may then show contrast behavior along all the dimensional lines represented by constructs which happen to have the mother as a symbol. This may be more than the therapist bargained for. The effect upon the client's construction of his life role may be disastrous. In this case we can hope that the client will have had enough independence of the therapist to reject the whole idea at the outset.

Consider the opposite kind of shift. Suppose we try to get the client to perceive and "accept" his likeness to his mother. We may think this is a matter of giving him a good dose of "insight."

In other words, what we are asking him to do is to see himself at the opposite end of *our* personal construct of *his mother* and we may be unaware of what such a shift implies in *his* personal construct of *his mother*. Our efforts may threaten to bring the client under the regnancy of all the construct poles for which *his mother* is his symbol.

Sometimes the therapist, in suggesting that a client is like his mother, has in mind only the idea that the client is like his mother *in some respect*. But the therapist may be overlooking the complex symbolic meaning of *mother* in the client's personal system. What the client then hears the therapist say is that he should identify himself with everything for which *mother* is the symbol. Yet the therapist may have meant only, "You get angry quickly like your mother," and not, "You are one of the mother-kind of people." After the client's mother has been relegated to her proper place as merely one of the contextual elements in a construct of *quick to anger* instead of being the quintessence of it, the client may be able to accept himself as representing one of the like elements in a context which also involves her. The process of lifting the symbolism from mother may require a considerable period of therapy, and yet it may have to precede any proffered interpretations or any significant therapeutic movement.

Suppose we attempt to shift the mother *as an element* from the like-self side of the context to the unlike-self side. This is usually an easy way to get an immediate appearance of movement. The client usually shows a lift of spirits, brightens up, and becomes more responsive. A conference or two later he may begin to show anxiety or reticence. As he begins to work through the implications of the shift, he may have found that his role has lost so much of its definition that it has ceased to provide him with a minimum level of personal security. The shift may have confused him. He cannot anticipate a regular enough sequence of life's events under the residual construction system.

What has happened in this case is that the client had previously become dependent upon the mother, not merely as the symbol for the role-governing construct of himself, but as the definition of it. It was her example which illustrated the construct in action.

The "lift" the client experienced when the shift was first proposed was essentially a freeing effect which appears, in this case, soon to have left him in an insecure position. This is a freedom which he cannot use until he has a construction within which it can operate in a way which will give him some preview of life. One has only to have experience in therapy with a child in a home which is in the process of breaking up in order to see this phenomenon in action. During the breakup period one or both of the parents is likely to try to dissociate the other from the like-self side of some of the child's personal role-governing constructs. The child faces freedom and insecurity through this enforced loss of his kinship with a role-exemplifying parent. It is quite understandable that the successful therapist in such a case will frequently find himself, instead, cast as the primary role exemplifier in the eyes of the child.

Last, let us consider the fourth kind of shift, still assuming that the client uses his mother-figure as the symbol of one of his role-governing constructs. Mother is to go from the unlike-self side to the like-self side. As in the immediately preceding case, this kind of shift also tends to destroy the construct's usefulness through the loss of its stabilizing symbol. In practice it appears to be impossible to retain the mother's symbolism when she is thus translated within the same construct. What usually happens is that the construct itself breaks up, or the client deals himself out as one of the like elements. In either case the role-governing features of the construct are likely to be lost. If the client reacts by dealing himself into the unlike pile, while retaining the construct itself, we have a situation on our hands similar to that discussed above in connection with a shift of the self to the unlike-mother side.

Now the symbol of a construct is usually one of the like elements, although that does not have to be the case. The mother figure can be one of the unlike elements and yet symbolize a construct maintained by the client. The client identifies himself with his mother's antitheses and these antitheses are the like elements. This is rare, but occasionally it actually happens in clinical work. It is, of course, not so rare that a person sees himself as unlike his mother; what is so rare is that the mother is at once the symbol of one of the client's role-governing constructs in which he is one of the like elements, yet she herself is one of the unlike elements. For example, his mother, by her bustling industry, may be the antithetical symbol of the very indolence with which the client identifies himself.

We have discussed in the preceding paragraphs of this section role-governing constructs which are maintained through figure-symbolism. We have used "mother" as the example of the figure-symbol in each instance. We have pointed out the disruptive effects upon the client's role when an attempt is made either to shift the self or the symbolizing figure in the context of the construct. What we have said is applicable to any contextual shifts in relation to a construct involving the self and a symbolizing figure. The use of a symbolizing figure gives the construct a kind of stability or rigidity. This may represent personal security for the child, or even for the adult whose construct system involves relatively few levels of abstraction and whose constructs must therefore be related directly to concrete behaviors or persons. Figure-symbolized constructs are characteristic of children. They lend clarity, and hence a measure of stability, to children's roles.

What we have said has some implications for psychotherapy which is carried out under the theoretical system of the psychology of personal constructs. Where figure symbolism is involved, or any symbolism for that matter, the self and the symbol cannot be shuffled with respect to each other without affecting the security provided by the construct. It may be necessary, and frequently is, for the therapist to help the client attach a new symbolism to his construct so that the element which was formerly the symbol can be shifted, or the self can be shifted with respect to it. If the symbol is a figure symbol — *mother*, for example — it may require a great deal of time and patience on the part of the therapist to replace the *mother* symbol, preparatory to bringing about shifts in the client's construction of his role. It may be more economical to start building a new set of constructs to replace the old altogether. In fixed-role therapy — to be discussed later — this is what is done.

Let us turn now to a more general case of personal security within the context of a construct. Let us disregard the symbolism of one of the elements. Let us disregard even the possibility that the self is the symbol of the construct. Consider only that the self is one of the elements. Now, since the construct is a way of holding its elements in place, the self is held in place by any construct by which the self is construed. The self-governing construct, or, more specifically where other people's presumed constructs are elements, the role-governing construct, provides a way of anticipating one's own responses. The result is social poise.

Consider an even more general case of personal security within the context of a construct. Let us disregard the possibility that the self is one of the elements. Consider only that the construct, perhaps having to do only with inanimate elements, provides a way of anticipating events. Armed with such a construct the person can face, not only his world of people, but his world of physical events with equanimity. This is an even broader kind of personal security. We might say that it represents personal poise.

14. DIMENSIONS OF CONSTRUCTS

The personal constructs of others may be construed by ourselves as observers. We can even set up comprehensive dimensions against which other persons' constructs can be evaluated. One of the common dimensions for evaluating constructs of others is the familiar *abstract vs. concrete* dimension. While there are some who believe that *abstract* is not the antithesis of *concrete,* most of us use these terms as if they represented the opposing poles of the same construct. We have, in our discussion thus far, had occasion to use these terms quite frequently, and we have been content to rely upon the usual meanings which readers might be expected to ascribe to them. But now it may be helpful to take a closer look at the nature of constructs and construe the various general ways in which constructs resemble and differ from each other.

Now constructs can be classified according to the elements

which they subsume. For example, a certain construct may be called a *physical* construct, not so much because it is subsumed within a "physical" system of constructs, but because it presumes to deal with elements which have already been construed as inherently "physical." Frequently the term *abstract* is used in this manner. For example, there are those who insist that any mathematical construct, regardless of who is using it, is bound to be "abstract" because it deals with symbols which have been defined as "abstract." But anyone who has done intensive psychodiagnostic work with scholarly people, including mathematicians, must have discovered that a man may be an excellent mathematician and yet actually handle his mathematics in a highly concretistic manner. There are some mathematicians who seem to have only the barest amount of capacity for abstract thinking. Their mathematical thinking is shot through with literalisms which are concretistic, legalistic, and scarcely abstract at all.

McGaughran has made a study in which he attempted to determine the functional usefulness of certain construct dimensions. He had not gone far before he realized that the classical scheme of *abstract vs. concrete* was not describing the thinking of his subjects in a manner that would enable him to predict how they would operate from one situation to another. The person who dealt abstractly with one kind of problem was as likely as not to deal concretely with another kind of problem. Furthermore, those who were more prone than others to use abstract approaches in one area might be less prone than others to use abstract approaches in another area.

McGaughran set for himself an experimental design in which he painstakingly sought to predict what kind of conceptualization a person would use in his language behavior from the kind he used in his nonverbal behavior, and vice versa. This was an ambitious undertaking. Language behavior was elicited by use of the Thematic Apperception Test cards. Nonverbal behavior was studied in the way the subject sorted the Vigotsky blocks. The task was to discover dimensions of conceptualization which would be applicable to both types of protocol and which would enable him to predict how a subject would perform in one situation from knowledge of his conceptualization in the other situation. In accepting this as his task he was introducing a functional criterion for the classification of constructs, certainly a novel idea in an area where philosophers have been accustomed to use only formalistic criteria.

McGaughran found eventually that he could make reasonably valid predictions and these predictions fell essentially in two dimensions. These were *communicability* and something which is essentially what we have been calling *permeability*. In fact, the term *permeability* was one originally suggested by Mc-Gaughran, although he did not choose to use it in reporting his study. By *communicability* he did not refer, of course, merely to verbal communication, since one set of protocols was, by definition, nonverbal. In other words, he found that the dimensions of *permeability* and *communicability* were not only operationally definable but were efficacious for predicting individual behavior. While we have not followed McGaughran's dimensional scheme precisely, we are indebted to him, not only for demonstrating that there are probably more meaningful ways to analyze conceptualization than by use of the *abstract-concrete* dimension, but also for suggesting certain definite features of constructs which may be far more characteristic of the users than is abstractness or concreteness.

In addition to the *permeability vs. impermeability* dimension, which has been discussed in an earlier section, we propose to use a triad of notions which basically represent two construct dimensions. These notions are not altogether unlike certain others which have been proposed by recent psychological writers. They have to do with the nature of the control which a construct implicitly exercises over its elements.

A construct which preempts its elements for membership in its own realm exclusively may be called a *preemptive construct.* The species type of construct belongs to this category. It can be exemplified by the statement, "Anything which is a ball can be nothing but a ball." In this case the construct is *ball,* and all the things which are balls are excluded from the realms of other constructs; they cannot be "spheres," "pellets," "shots," or anything but balls. This is a pigeonhole type of construct; what has been put into this pigeonhole cannot simultaneously be put into any other. It represents, of course, the extreme of preemption and actually few personal constructs are totally preemptive in their use. Yet in therapy the tendency of the client to use preemptive construction in dealing with certain topical areas is often a major problem for the therapist. The problem of preemption is also a major factor in interpersonal relations and in certain thick-skulled approaches to social conflict. But more of this later.

Preemption tends to show up in those who have particular difficulty in seeing the universe as an ongoing affair and insist that dealing with it is simply a matter of arranging its inert elements. The pre-Aristotelian philosopher Heraclitus had actually made a pretty good start in construing an active universe, which he could see epitomized in fire. But the import of what he had to say was masked by the substantialism of philosophers like Empedocles, and it was lost altogether when Aristotle put science into pigeonholes and refused to countenance anything so dynamic as the performance of an experiment, lest it be a distortion of nature.

During the past century there has been some recovery from the preemptiveness of Aristotelian thinking and greater emphasis upon the functional approaches to reality. Dewey, whose philosophy and psychology can be read between many of the lines of the psychology of personal constructs, envisioned the universe as an ongoing affair which had to be anticipated to be understood. Such thinking stands in sharp contrast to the kind of realism which insists that if a thing is a spade, it is nothing but a spade: if a person is a schizophrenic, he is nothing but a schizophrenic; if the heart is a physiological organ, it is nothing but a physiological organ, and it cannot be construed as a psychological organ; if an event is a catastrophe, it is nothing but a catastrophe; if a man is an enemy, he is nothing but an enemy.

Preemptive construction is often exemplified in the polemic disputes between scientists. It is sometimes called the *nothing-but* criticism: "The psychology of personal constructs is *nothing but* mentalism"; "Psychoanalysis is *nothing but* anthropomorphism"; "Christianity is *nothing but* passivity"; "Communism is *nothing but* dictatorship." When we laid down our basic position in terms of constructive alternativism we eschewed the nothing-but type of reasoning from the outset, and we played the hunch that the abandonment of this kind of outlook might do a great deal to help psychologists along, just as it often helps their clients to reconstrue life and find renewed hope among stark realities.

A construct which permits its elements to belong to other realms concurrently, but fixes their realm memberships, may be called a *constellatory construct*. A stereotype belongs to this category. For example, a constellatory construct is expressed in the statement, "Anything which is a ball must also be something which will bounce." Some investigators call this a "complex." In this type of construct it is conceded that a ball may also be considered as something other than a ball, but there is no latitude permitted as to what else it may be considered to be. A ball, if a ball, has to be certain specified other things too.

A construct which leaves its elements open to construction in all other respects may be called a *propositional construct*. For example, throughout our discussion of the psychology of personal constructs we have attempted to rely heavily upon propositional constructs, as contrasted with the entity thinking implied by the use of preemptive constructs and the dogmatic thinking implied by the use of constellatory constructs. In the case of the ball example the following illustrates a propositional construct: "Any roundish mass may be considered, among other things, as a ball." Such a construct is relatively propositional since it does not hinge upon anything except the "roundish mass" and it does not imply that a ball has to be any particular thing except a "roundish mass." In personal thinking such pure abstraction is about as rare as the utter concretism implied in preemptive construction. The propositional construct, therefore, represents one end of a continuum, the other end of which is represented by the preemptive and constellatory constructs.

While propositionality may seem to be a universally desirable characteristic in one's personal constructs, it would actually be quite difficult to get along in the world if a person attempted to use propositional constructs exclusively. A superordinate construct, which subsumes other constructs, treats its subordinates as if they were constellatory. For example, if *sphere* includes *ball* together with certain other objects, then to say that something is a ball is also to imply that it is a sphere. Thus *ball* has a constellatory implication when it is subsumed by *sphere*.

Moreover, if a person attempted to use propositional thinking exclusively, he might have considerable difficulty in coming to any decision as to what the relevant and crucial issues were in any situation. In a game of baseball he might be so busy considering, from all conceptual angles, the sphere which was being thrown in his direction that he might overlook the necessity for dealing with it momentarily as a ball and nothing else. Preemptive thinking, in a moment of decision, is essential if one is to take an active part in his universe. But preemptive thinking which never resolves itself into propositional thinking condemns the person to a state of intellectual rigor mortis. He may be called a "man of action," but his actions will always follow well-worn ruts.

We can summarize as follows what we have to say at this point about the dimensions of constructs:

a. *An impermeable construct* is one which is based upon a specified context and which will admit no additional elements — for example, proper names: "If *ball* comprises certain things, then no other things can be balls"; "These and these only are balls."

b. *A permeable construct* is one which implies additional elements — for example, class names: "If *ball* comprises certain things, then there must be still other things which are balls"; "Anything like these is a ball."

c. *A preemptive construct* is one which preempts its elements for membership in its own realm exclusively — for example, species names: "Anything which is a ball can be nothing but a ball"; "This is nothing but a ball."

d. *A constellatory construct* is one which fixes the realm membership of its elements — for example, stereotypes: "Anything which is a ball has got to be . . . " "Since this is a ball, it must be round, resilient, and small enough to hold in the hand."

e. *A propositional construct* is one which does not disturb the other realm memberships of its elements — for example, "philosophical attitudes": "Any roundish mass can be considered, among other things, as a ball"; "Although this is a ball, there is no reason therefore to believe that it could not be lopsided, valuable, or have a French accent."

Later on we propose to list many more dimensional lines along which personal constructs may be plotted. *Anxiety, hostility, loosening, preverbalism, transference, dependence,* and a number of other dimensions will be described. But we are eager to finish our preliminary sketch of the psychology of personal constructs, so that, as soon as possible, we may demonstrate some of the theory's more interesting practical applications to the solution of human problems. Further dimensions will have to wait!

C. Changing Construction

15. VALIDATION

When we laid down our Fundamental Postulate we committed ourselves to a particular view of human motivation. *A person's processes are psychologically channelized by the ways in which he anticipates events.* The direction of his movement, hence his motivation, is toward better understanding of what will happen. Where Dewey would have said that we understand events through anticipating them, we would add that our lives are wholly oriented toward the anticipation of events. The person moves out toward making more and more of the world predictable and not ordinarily does he withdraw more and more into a predictable world. In the latter case he becomes neurotic or psychotic, lest he lose that capacity for prediction which he has already acquired. In either case, the principle of the elaborative choice describes his motivating decision. Moreover, as we have indicated before, he lays his wagers on predictability, not merely on the certainty of the immediate venture, but in terms of what he sees as the best parlay. Often, too, he finds it necessary to compromise between comprehensiveness and specific accuracy in his construction system. Thus he may tolerate an obviously misleading construct in his system if it seems to have the comprehensiveness that a more precise construct appears to lack.

If man is concerned primarily with the anticipation of events, we need no longer appeal to hedonism, or some disguised form of it, such as "satisfaction" or "reinforcement," to explain his behavior. We can, of course, redefine some hedonistic terms in the language of prediction and validation, and thus continue to use them — but why bother!

What follows from our Fundamental Postulate is a particular notion of the kind of pay-off man expects from his wagers. Let us use the term *validation*. A person commits himself to anticipating a particular event. If it takes place, his anticipation is validated. If it fails to take place, his anticipation is invalidated. Validation represents the compatibility (subjectively construed) between one's prediction and the outcome he observes. Invalidation represents incompatibility (subjectively construed) between one's prediction and the outcome he observes.

Sometimes the client in therapy will construe as invalidation of a prediction what the therapist has expected him to construe as validation. Sometimes this happens because the therapist is not fully aware of the nature of the client's prediction. Sometimes it occurs because the therapist construes prediction and outcome at a sufficiently comprehensive level to see them as compatible with each other, but the client, not having such an overview, is disturbed because he won $998.14 on his wager instead of the $998.00 he expected to win.

The notion of *validation* is quite different from the notion of "reinforcement," as the latter term is commonly used. Reinforcement carries the implication of meeting the person's needs, of satisfying him in some way, or of gratification. Validation refers solely to the verification of a prediction, even though what was predicted was something unpleasant. For example, a person may anticipate that he will fall down the stairs and break his leg. If his prediction turns out to be true, or at least if it seems to him that he has fallen down the stairs and broken his leg, he experiences validation, no matter how unhappy he may be about the turn of affairs. But breaking one's leg is ordinarily not what one would call "reinforcement," except, possibly, in certain disturbed patients. Of course, we could redefine "reinforcement" to bring it into line with the theory of personal constructs; but most of the current meaning that "reinforcement" has among psychologists would then have to be abandoned.

When a prediction turns out to be accurate, what is it which is validated? If it turns out to be inaccurate, what is invalidated? These are questions which assume considerable importance in the psychology of personal constructs. While they are, in some measure, important also in most of the current learning theories which deal with generalization, the psychology of personal constructs casts them in a somewhat different light.

Poch's research deals with this problem. She structured the issues in this way: when a person discovers that his prediction has gone awry, just what does he do about it? Does he change his prediction only? Does he turn to another construct in his repertory and base his next prediction on that instead? Or does he revise the dimensional structure of his construct system?

Conventional learning theory, based on the notion of "reinforcement," normally concerns itself only with the first of these questions. Available research evidence indicates clearly enough that persons ordinarily do change their predictions when they find that they have made mistakes. But Poch's questions penetrate much deeper than this. Her evidence indicated quite clearly that her subjects tended to turn to other construct dimensions in their repertories when their predictions were invalidated. There was also a tendency for them to shift their construct system with respect to the aspects employed in the invalidated predictions.

We may see, then, that validation can be viewed as affecting the construction system at various levels. These levels can be seen as falling into gradients, with those constructs which are functionally closest to the constructs upon which the original prediction was based being most affected by validational experiences. Bieri has shown how this relationship can be measured, both for constructs and for figures in the person's life. He has shown how validation affects not only the particular constructs and the particular figures which were involved in the original prediction, but also affects functionally related constructs and figures.

Our Experience Corollary infers from the Fundamental Postulate that a person's construction system varies as he successively construes the replications of events. Validation points off the successive cycles in his construing. If a person makes only vague commitments to the future he receives only vague validational experience. If his commitments are incidental and fragmentary, he experiences fragmentary validation only. If his commitments are based on far-reaching interpretations of the situation, he may construe the outcome as having sweeping significance.

This kind of reasoning gives us an approach to the results of the so-called "partial conditioning" experiments. It has been demonstrated variously that a "response" will resist "extinction" under conditions of "nonreinforcement" longer if, during the original "conditioning" period, not all of the "trials" were "reinforced." This is somewhat awkward for most of the conventional learning theories to explain. From our point of view, however, it suggests that the validational cycle — from prediction to outcome — is not necessarily the single "trial" as envisioned by the experimenter. The "trial," from the subject's point of view, may be a cycle of several "trials," from the experimenter's point of view. Just because the experimenter phrases his experience in a certain way is no reason for the subject to phrase it in the same way. Thus the partially "reinforced" series may, from the standpoint of the subject, consist of a number of different cycles, all of which were "reinforced," but some of which were longer than others. Even the total experimental series itself may be a cycle, as far as the subject is concerned, and it may be that he will give up making his prediction only when the "extinction" series approaches, subjectively, the length of the "conditioning" series — that is, from where the subject considered that the cycle began to where the subject considered that he received his terminal validation. Again, as we have suggested before, it is often more helpful to discover what the subject has learned rather than whether or not he conforms to what the experimenter has learned.

16. CONDITIONS FAVORABLE TO THE FORMATION OF NEW CONSTRUCTS

At the end of the section on the personal construction of one's role, we pointed out that new constructs can be formed with less danger of paralyzing effects if they are first approached in contexts which do not involve the client's self or members of his immediate family. In the section on personal security within the context of a construct we pointed out the disruption of one's role that may result from attempts to change certain figure elements in a construct when the construct is a role-governing construct and one of the figures — the mother-figure, for example — is the symbol of the construct. We suggested that in some cases it may be more economical to start from scratch and help the client form a new set of role-governing constructs altogether. Thus a person might first develop a new hypothetical cast of characters and only later find that they were like the people with whom he is living every day.

a. *Use of fresh elements.* In the first place, it is helpful if a fresh set of elements is provided as the context in which a new construct is to emerge. The elements, being relatively unbound by old constructs which would be seen as being incompatible with the new construct, do not involve the person with the old constructs until he has brought the new into a state of usefulness. In the common language of psychotherapists, "resistance is temporarily circumvented." This procedure includes such safeguards as developing new constructs in contexts which do not involve the self or members of the immediate family. It includes setting up a therapy situation which, at first, is insular as far as the rest of the client's world is concerned. The sanitarium or the private therapy room may provide the "protected environment" so frequently mentioned in connection with psychotherapy. A therapist who is previously unknown to the client and who does not let himself become too fixed a figure in the client's world is an important fresh element upon which the client can start to develop wholly new constructs. In setting up fresh elements the therapist must be careful, however, not to introduce the client to so complicated a new world that he cannot make his moment-to-moment anticipations work at all. Even though the situation is insular, it must not be implausible.

There are various ways of developing new constructs upon fresh verbal elements. The development of tailor-made and carefully designed stories is a powerful tool in child psychotherapy and one which, incidentally, has amazingly escaped systematic treatment by psychologists. The reading of Hawthorne's *The Great Stone Face* should suggest psychotherapeutic procedures beyond those which are commonly employed. We are familiar with the social-controlling effect of folklore, so important in the understanding of cultural anthropology; it is only a short step from folklore to the use of similar stories for special therapeutic purposes. In the clinical experience of the writer it has been relatively easy to develop new constructs for children in connection with story elements and thus give them form, definition, and usefulness before they come into conflict with the constructs which they are eventually to replace. In the use of stories the self is only gradually involved and the new constructs which are developed are allowed to replace only gradually those undesirable role constructs which have continued to exercise control in the client's life after having outlived their validity.

The composition and playing out of artificial roles, as elements upon which to create new constructs which in turn are later to have more vital meanings, is another example of the use of fresh elements to develop new constructs. The patent artificiality of the role is the very feature which prevents the tender shoots of new ideas from being trampled in the frantic rush to maintain oneself in his previous role.

b. *Experimentation.* The next condition which is hospitable to the formation of new constructs is an atmosphere of experimentation. In more precise language this means the shifting of construct grounds upon which predictions are based and the checking of validating experiences to see which anticipations have corresponded to actual outcomes. It means even more. It means that the constructs are tried out in relative isolation from each other; this corresponds to the scientist's use of experimental controls. Constellatory constructs, as we have described them in a previous section, are tentatively avoided. The atmosphere of experimentation is one in which the consequences of one's experimental acts are seen as limited. One does not "play for keeps." Constructs, in the true scientific tradition, are seen as "being tried on for size." They are seen propositionally. In fact, the seeing of constructs as proposed representations of reality rather than the reality itself is propaedeutic to experimentation.

The client who is to form new constructs is encouraged to "try out" new behaviors or to explore within a controlled situation, perhaps verbally only, the outcomes of asymptotic behavior. His tentative constructions of the roles of other people may be tried out on the therapist. In the language of psychoanalysis this is "transference." Later we shall attempt to give *transference* an operational definition. At the moment it is sufficient to consider transference as a special case of experimentation with role constructs.

c. *Availability of validating data.* The third condition which is hospitable to the formation of new constructs is the availability of validating data. A construct is a framework for making predictions. If it does not work, there is a tendency to alter it — within the more permeable aspects of the construction system, of course. If returns on the prediction are unavailable or unduly delayed, one is likely to postpone changing the construct under which the prediction was made.

In the field of applied learning it has long been pointed out that "knowledge of results facilitates learning." This has been substantiated on a research basis. It needs rather careful interpretation, however. What the experimenter sees as "results" may not be what the subject in the learning experiment sees as "results." If the subject is checking the results of his thinking within the larger aspects of his system, he may not consider the experimenter's "results" as relevant.

Suppose a subject is attempting to solve a puzzle. He puts certain blocks together, knowing full well that eventually they cannot go together in that particular sequence, in order to get an idea of what the eventual volume of the completed puzzle will be like. He is developing an intermediate construct. The experimenter, with his forefinger on the phrase, "knowledge of results," keeps nagging the subject by telling him that his "trials" are unsuccessful. This is an instance in which the phrasing of the process for the subject is different from what it is for the experimenter. For the subject, the "trials," as he sees them, may be "successful." This point has been previously mentioned in connection with the phrasing of experience.

Rather than throwing the emphasis upon knowledge of preconceived results, we have chosen to throw the emphasis upon availability of results in general as a facilitating condition for the formation of new constructs. In this manner the subject is permitted to phrase his experience in different ways. If he wishes to make long-range predictions, he is not plagued with moment-by-moment "outcomes." If he wishes to make a long-term investment, he is not compelled to keep reading ticker tape. If he wishes to develop intermediate constructs or "tools," the fact that he is not yet anticipating the eventual outcomes successfully will not need to be interpreted as invalidating his efforts.

In the psychotherapeutic situation the availability of validating data implies skill on the part of the therapist. For the most part, this is verbal skill in expressing clearly facts and reactions, against which the client can check the results of his explorations whenever he is ready to do so. The therapist has to guard himself against producing facts which serve no purpose except to provide further confirmation of those constructs which ought to be replaced. Sometimes the client will ask, "Don't you agree that my wife is impossible?" This is one the clinician will probably duck! Even if the clinician agreed, his agreement might not properly be considered as validating data for the construct the client really had in mind, although it would probably be construed in that way.

The clinician needs to be continually alert as to what constructs are being "tried on," and try to govern the availability of data in terms of what is relevant to the construct actually being used. The client's question in the above paragraph may be indicative of various constructs other than the one explicitly expressed. For example, it may be interpreted to mean, "I'm not such a bad husband, am I?" It may mean, "You will help protect me from my wife, won't you?" It may mean, "You are a better friend than my wife, aren't you?" It may mean, "Everything will be all right if I get rid of my wife, won't it?" If a clinician gives an answer, it is a good thing for him to know what question he is answering. That, of course, is not always possible.

Sometimes clinicians like to emphasize "objectivity." They keep confronting the client with "facts," in the hope that a continual steeping in such "truthful" material will give the poor fellow a proper flavor. They usually succeed only in keeping the client in a stew. Many a clinician, under the guise of objectivity, gives his clients the "right" answers to the wrong questions. In other words, "objectivity" is altogether too frequently a disguise for literalism, and hence is not objective at all, merely verbal.

The role-playing exchange is an excellent way of enabling the client to try out new constructs which have immediate access to validating material. If it is carried out as a rehearsal, he has a preliminary round of validating data. If it is tried out in an extramural situation, he may have even more impressive evidence regarding the efficacy of this new construct.

The offering of interpretations of the client's attitudes of transference is an example of the use of validating data in the verification or falsification of constructs. The client tries out both old and new role constructs upon the therapist; the therapist both clarifies them and, by implication, makes it clear that, as regards some of them, appropriate results are not to be anticipated from them in any situation other than a childlike or a clinical one.

By providing validating data in the form of responses to a wide variety of constructions on the part of the client, some of them quite loose, fanciful, or naughty, the clinician gives the client an opportunity to validate constructs, an opportunity which is not normally available to him. This, of course, involves a good deal more than "setting the patient right about things" or "preaching." It involves a careful prior analysis of the client's personal constructs and an opportunity for him to work them out in explicit forms. Again, it must be a way of giving the right answers to the right questions rather than the literal answers to the wrong questions.

It will be in order to say much more about the optimal conditions for the formation of new and regnant constructs when we discuss the techniques of psychotherapy. The preceding discussion is intended merely to be illustrative of the basic requirements involved in the propagation of new constructs.

17. CONDITIONS UNFAVORABLE TO THE FORMATION OF NEW CONSTRUCTS

In general a failure to maintain conditions favorable to the formation of new constructs will delay their formation. There are, however, certain conditions which are especially inimical to the formation of new constructs. The most important of these is that in which the elements out of which the new construct is to be formed involve *threat*.

a. *Threat*. First, let us state rather precisely what we mean by *threat*. Basically, *threat* is a characteristic of a construct's relation to the superordinate constructs in a system. A construct is threatening when it is itself an element in a next-higher-order construct which is, in turn, incompatible with other higher-order constructs upon which the person is dependent for his living. The construct of danger is a *threat* when it becomes an element in the context of death or injury. There are circumstances when it is not a threat, at least not a very significant one. A roller-coaster elicits a construct of danger, but that danger is rarely placed in the context of death.

To continue our illustration: death, of course, is incompatible with living, at least in the minds of most people. There are people, however, who do not see life and death as incompatible. One may see death as an entrance to a phase of life beyond the River Styx. One may see death merely as a vestibule through which transmigration of the soul takes place. If death is incompatible with the construction system through which one maintains a basic orientation toward events and their anticipation, then the like elements in the context of death are threats. We shall have much more to say about threat later, for it is an important construct in the clinician's repertory.

Now if the elements out of which it is proposed to form a new construct commonly involve threat, that is, if they tend to elicit a construct or an issue which is basically incompatible with the system upon which the person has come to rely for his living — he may not readily utilize the elements for forming any new construct. The interpretation which makes them threatening may not even be as serious a matter as death. Its mere incompatibility with the construction system upon which one leans heavily in any way may make its elements threatening.

One may ask why a particular client is so insistent in construing the elements in such a way as to make them threats. The answer to this lies in the inherent nature of constructs themselves. One maintains his construct system by clarifying it. Even one's own system is stabilized or controlled in the manner in which outside events are controlled. This means, among other things, that one controls his system by maintaining a clear identification of the elements which the system excludes as well as those which it includes. The moment one finds himself becoming involved in any way with the excluded elements of his system, he becomes aware of the onset of incompatibility and sees these new clutching associations as threats. Like a wounded animal, he keeps facing his enemy.

Now what happens when the client is presented with new elements which seek to ally themselves with his self in the formation of an intolerable construct? He may seek to disperse them or, as a last resort, he may turn his whole attention to the extrication of himself from the unholy alliance and to the rejection of the new elements in one big lump. The clinician can see this happen before his eyes. It is the very plausibility of the unwanted elements which makes them a threat to the person. If they seemed utterly alien to him, he would not be threatened by them; he could assume the part of a bystander.

It is clear that this kind of reaction to elements which are proposed as a basis for formulating new constructs would make them useless to their purpose. The effect of threat is to compel the client to claw frantically for his basic construct. Threat arouses the necessity for mobilizing one's resources. It should be borne in mind that the resources which are mobilized may not always be mature and effective. Therefore a threatened person may often behave in childish ways.

Another effect of introducing threatening elements, and frequently an undesirable one, is the tendency for the traumatic experience to act as further subjective documentation or proof of the client's own maladaptive conceptual framework. Not only may the traumatized client be thrown back upon older and more infantile constructions of life, but he is likely, through this further experience, to find "proof" of those primitive constructions. It is correct to say of traumatic experience that it usually "freezes people in their tracks." It is important for the clinician to assess the freezing effect that may result from the introduction of certain new material in a therapy session.

b. *Preoccupation with old material.* There is another condition which is inimical to the formation of new constructs. That is an exclusive preoccupation with old material — what happens when a client in a psychotherapeutic series becomes unduly repetitive. Then the therapist begins to complain to his colleagues that he can see no movement. Old or familiar material tends to be fixed in place by old and childlike constructs; it is only as we let the client interweave it with new and adult material that he starts bringing his constructs up to date. The interlarding of new material with the old calls for new sorting of old material into new categories that will fit both the old and the new material.

Sometimes old constructs are impermeable. The events they subsume are the last of their kind. Such constructs are practically of no use in dealing with future events, and it may be just as well for the client that they are that way. In certain types of psychotic patients it may be desirable to let an old delusion lapse into impermeability rather than trying to resolve it by reconstruing the events it subsumes. The same may be true with respect to the outmoded but inaccessible constructs that one finds occasionally in less disturbed clients.

Sometimes one makes a deliberate effort to reduce a client's construct to a state of inoperative impermeability. Basically this is what happens in the establishment of a habit. The habit becomes a way of dealing with old material, but it certainly is not an alert way of dealing directly with new elements. There is nothing open-ended about a habitualized construct. That is not to say that habits are useless in helping one deal with the onrush of events. They do serve the purpose of stabilizing certain constructions so that one may be left otherwise free to deal intelligently, by contrast, with selected aspects of the new material. A habit may be considered as a convenient kind of stupidity which leaves a person free to act intelligently elsewhere. Whether he takes advantage of the opportunity or not is another question. Some people fail to seize the advantages offered them by their stupidity.

c. *No laboratory.* New constructs are not formed when one lacks a laboratory in which to try them out. This is just as true of any person as it is true of the scientist. A laboratory is a situation in which there is present, for the person to re-sort, a sufficient amount of the stuff out of which new constructs can be formed. It is difficult to form new social concepts out of situations which are barren of social relationships. It is difficult to form new parental constructs out of a situation which involves no parents. It is impossible to teach a prisoner who has had no relations with women for years how to play his sex role properly. It is impossible for a hospitalized patient to learn social poise in a situation which denies him the opportunity to assume a dignified position. A soldier, denied the privileges of democracy, learns little of how it operates — this, even though he may yearn for its advantages.

A laboratory also provides a convenient insulation from other variables, the complexities of which might swamp the person who is trying to form new constructs in a necessarily limited sphere. If one considers at once all the ramifications and ultimate consequences of each exploratory act, he will be overwhelmed and unable to formulate any new construct. One who has directed graduate students in their research efforts will have frequently seen this kind of intellectual drowning take place. Frequently the student sees so many implications of his study and so many possible variables to be considered that he is unable to design his experiment. A laboratory, however, permits a person to explore in a limited sphere. The bang that results from some of his inadvertent mixtures need not blow up his world. This is a way of saying what we have already said before on the affirmative side: that a person who is completely and continually involved in the ultimate consequences of his acts is in no position to experiment with new ideas.

Like the scientist who must form testable hypotheses and then try them out, the person who is to form new hypotheses needs to have data available in a form which his new constructs will either predict or clearly fail to predict. The person who lives in a completely elastic world can soon become discouraged in his attempts to measure it. The child whose parents are predictable only within a framework which is too complex for him to understand lives in such a world. He may be as maladjusted with respect to his parents as is the child whose parents would make all of his social constructs impermeable ones, or, to use the psychoanalytic notion, who attempt to organize all of his relations with them under "superego" control.

D. The Meaning of Experience

18. THE CONSTRUED NATURE OF EXPERIENCE

By now the reader is fully aware that the psychology of personal constructs sets itself against some strong currents in the main stream of psychological thought. Ours is an *anticipatory* rather than a *reactive* system. To many it will seem that we have herein abandoned a basic tenet of all modern science.

At the heart of this heresy is the delicate question of how a system such as ours is to deal with *experience*. Indeed, how does the person himself deal with experience? Is not man a product of his experience? Can he do other than *react* to it? Are not one's personal constructs always prefabricated by the disembodied hands of his culture? Let us see.

There is a world which is happening all the time. Our experience is that portion of it which is happening to us. These two thoughts may be combined into the simple philosophical statement, "The universe is existing and man is coming to know it."

In the sections immediately preceding this one, we have concerned ourselves with the knowing process; now let us turn our attention to that which is known.

Things happen to us personally only when we behave in relation to them. But we have already committed ourselves to the position that psychological response is initially and basically the outcome of a construing act. Experience, therefore, in this system, must be defined as the compass of fact which has fallen within a man's purview. It is a set of personally construed events. To study a man's experience, then, is to have a look at that upon which, rightly or wrongly, he has placed some construction.

Experience is the extent of what we know — up to now. It is not necessarily valid. We may "know" a lot of things which are untrue, like the naval officer who was once described by a distinguished psychologist as having been gifted with a vast and versatile ignorance. Knowing things is a way of letting them happen to us. The unfortunate naval officer simply had allowed a lot of things to happen to him in a peculiar way. He had *variety of experience*, but his constructions were invalid. If his personal constructs continued to mislead him, he could be expected to sink a lot of whales and shoot down a lot of more or less friendly Air Force planes. But he had experience!

Just as the compass of experience is no guarantee of the validity of our personal constructs, neither does the *duration of experience* give us any such warranty. There is the case of the veteran school administrator, described by Dean Arthur Klein of Ohio State University, who had "had only one year of experience — repeated thirteen times." In this statement there is the implication that it is only the sequence of the construing process which gives both added range to one's experience and more comprehensive validity to one's anticipations. Presumably, the administrator, during his successive years of service, had not enlarged the scope of his vision or diminished the reaches of his misinformation.

Our Experience Corollary claims that a person's construction system varies as he successively construes the replications of events. If he fails to reconstrue events, even though they keep repeating themselves, he minimizes his experience. The person who takes events for granted, and who does not seek new light to throw upon them, adds very little to his store of experience as the years go on. Sometimes it is said that a person learns from experience. From the standpoint of the psychology of personal constructs, however, it is the learning which constitutes experience.

It is interesting to note the effect that reconstruing has upon the range of one's experience. Our Modulation Corollary states that the variation in a person's construction system is limited by the permeability of the constructs within whose ranges of convenience the variants lie. This is a matter of taking events in one's stride. If he tries to deal with his world by legalistic bookkeeping, he is likely to find that there is little he can do to adapt himself to varying events. A person who approaches his world with a repertory of impermeable constructs is likely to find his system unworkable through the wider expanses of events. He will, therefore, tend to constrict his experience to the narrower ranges which he is prepared to understand. On the other hand, if he is prepared to perceive events in new ways, he may accumulate experience rapidly. It is this adaptability which provides a more direct measure of the growing validity of a man's construct system than does the amount of time he consumes in swatting at the events which buzz around his ears.

To summarize, our experience is that portion of the universe which is happening to us — that is, which is successively construed by us — and the increase of experience is a function, not of the hodgepodge of events which we have construed, or of the time spent in being aware of them, but of the successive revision of our construct system in the general direction of increased validity. An analysis of experience, then, becomes a study of the field of fact which one has segmented into meaningful events; the way those events, in turn, are construed; the kinds of evidence against which one has checked the validity of his predictions; the progressive changes which the constructs have undergone; and, most of all, the more permeable and durable constructs which have subsumed the whole evolvement.

19. THE INTERPRETATION OF EXPERIENCE

Up to this point we have not developed any public diagnostic constructs for the clinician's use. This comes in a later chapter. Before we propose such constructs we want to discuss further man's experience and the personal way he structures it. We also want to illustrate how man can recover from his experiences, as, for example, in psychotherapy. The diagnostic constructs we propose need to be designed in relation to such recovery.

So far our approach to personal constructs has been almost phenomenological or descriptive. Yet our theoretical position is not strictly phenomenological, for we recognize that personal constructs locked up in privacy cannot be made the subject of a book designed for public consumption. What we attempt to do is to lift our data from the individual at a relatively high level of abstraction. This is a little like saying that we deal concretely with a person's abstractions rather than abstractly with his concretisms. Behaviorism, for example, did it the other way; it created elaborate public abstractions out of minute personal concretisms.

In practice, what we do is observe the individual's behaviors, using the lowest possible common denominators of description. Then, continuing to deal descriptively with the individual, we observe his personal abstractions of those behaviors — his *constructs*. Now these abstractions are not necessarily verbalized by him, nor are they necessarily immediately translatable by him into verbalizations, either in the public language or in his own babble. His abstractions of his own behavior may be structured or construed by him solely in terms of anticipated continuities and cycles. They are still abstractions. They are isolated. There is still a construct-like discrimination of simultaneous likeness and difference in the way he thinks about them.

Now the personal-construct psychologist observes a person's own abstractions of behavior, both as they are verbalized and as they are otherwise regularized by the individual. But the personal-construct psychologist initially deals with them as concretely, from his own point of view, as possible. He starts by taking what he sees and hears at face value. He even takes at face value what he sees and hears about his subject's constructs. In psychotherapy this is commonly called "acceptance" of the client. For Sullivan it would be "learning the language of the patient." Our term, which we shall elaborate later, is *the credulous attitude.*

But the psychologist is himself a person; hence, his psychological processes follow his own personal constructs. Other psychologists are persons too. If there is to be a common understanding of the client, there must be commonality in the way he is construed. If there is to be a constructive social process involving the client — for example, therapy — the person who is to play the role of therapist must subsume the constructs of the subject rather than merely interpret his overt behavior. All of this means that we cannot consider the psychology of personal constructs a phenomenological theory, if that means ignoring the personal construction of the psychologist who does the observing.

What the personal-construct psychologist does is first attempt to describe accurately the highest levels of abstraction in his subject's system at the lowest possible levels of abstraction in his own. This is what we meant when we said that data should be lifted at a relatively high level of abstraction. We were referring to a high level of abstraction *in the subject's system.* This could not, of course, have been taken to mean that the data themselves were to be considered as abstractions in the system in which they were handled by the psychologist. Data, when considered as such by the psychologist, are relatively concrete elements awaiting some sort of construction.

20. THE AHISTORICAL APPROACH

The perceptual theories in psychology are frequently said to espouse the ahistorical approach to the understanding of behavior. This approach is from the viewpoint that one's activity at a given moment is determined primarily by his outlook at that moment. What has actually happened in the past can influence behavior only through the perceptions which are operating at the present instant. Personal-construct theory takes a somewhat similar stand. In personal-construct theory, however, the basis of perception has been broadened to include "nonconscious" as well as "conscious" processes, and the manner of perception has been cast in the form of *constructs*.

It should be emphasized, also, that personal-construct theory does not ignore history, just as some perceptual theories do not actually ignore history even though they may consider it a remote rather than an immediate determinant of behavior. Now history, as contrasted with chronology, is a method of study, not a definitive set of causes. In personal-construct theory one may be interested in a historical type of study because it helps to reveal the successive patterning of the elements for whose interpretation his client's personal constructs are formed. Sometimes it is only through the analysis of these elements that we can infer what the client's presently operating constructs must be like. This is a legitimate psychological use of the *historical method*. It is granted that our use of the method is indirect, and thus is in contrast with the direct approaches illustrated in the last chapter, but there are occasions when one must utilize such indirect ways of gaining access to personal constructs.

21. GROUP EXPECTANCIES AS VALIDATORS OF PERSONAL CONSTRUCTS

Among the many kinds of events in the world which one seeks to anticipate optimally, people and their behaviors are particularly salient. People, too, are events. One can have a set of constructs whose contexts comprise other persons as elements. The elements can also be specific bits of behavior of the other persons. When one tries such a construct on for size he subjects it to a process of validation. If his friends behave the way he expects them to behave, he accumulates supportive evidence for his construct; if they do not, his construct has, in this one instance, failed to provide him with a precise anticipation of events.

This failure, of course, does not necessarily mean that a person will immediately discard his construct. The construct may, considering all of its elements, and not merely the single unfortunate event which has just been concluded, still provide him with what he considers to be an optimal basis for predicting the behavior of most persons. In the long run, however, he must come to accept the total accumulation of evidence — or what he construes as evidence — which attests to the validity or invalidity of the construct under which he has been operating. In the case of constructs involving people, this evidence is the subsequent behavior of the people with whom he comes in contact.

But let us take into account the fact that the behavior which is taken as validating evidence is also itself psychologically generated. "Other people" are persons too. They, in turn, act according to their anticipations. When one lives in a community in which the commonality of personal constructs is extensive, one finds people behaving similarly because they tend to expect the same things. In this sense, the expectancies which are common to the group actually operate as the validators against which the individual tends to verify the predictive efficiency of his own constructs. Broadly, this is what we mean by saying that group expectancies are validators of personal constructs.

There are some special cases of the way in which group expectancies operate as validators of personal constructs. First, let us consider a type of construct which is not about people at all, but for which the validating evidence is *ordinarily* available only by way of other people's opinions. Take, for example, the construct of *sphericity,* as applied to the earth. While certain features of curvature can be observed directly at sea, we are, for the most part, dependent upon other people's descriptions of their own experience for evidence of the earth's complete sphericity. If the people with whom we come in contact all expect the earth to be as flat as a pancake, all the validating evidence to which we must subject our construct of earth sphericity is negative. We may have to decide that the earth is flat after all. This is a particular type of case in which the opinions of other people operate as validators of one's personal constructs about nonhuman events.

Next, let us consider the case of the person who is construed by his neighbors in such a way that he is always expected to do certain things. Whenever he fails to perform according to their expectations he finds them acting as if he had threatened them. He has. Now he may start to fancy himself as an unpredictable person — unpredictable, that is, for other people. In that case he may go right on shocking the neighbors. His conceptualization of himself, at the same time, is markedly affected. In order to maintain his pose he may have to construe himself as a "shocking" person. Thus, even though he rejects the expectancies of his neighbors as being invalid, he has had to construe himself in relation to those expectancies and has had to bring his behavior under the reign of constructs which are carefully validated in reverse of his neighbors' expectancies.

This kind of perverse conformity can frequently be observed in children. A child attempts to establish himself in relation to his parents. He may do this by being negativistic. Yet, in order to be consistently negativistic, he must see the world the way his parents see it. Only by doing so can he be sure to place himself at the contrast pole of each of their constructs. He winds up using the very same dimensional system his parents use.

A third special way in which group expectancies may be considered as validators of personal constructs involves one's construction of his role. *Role*, as we have tried to define it in a strict sense, was not necessarily involved in the example of the person who tried so hard to behave in contrast to his neighbors' expectations that he adopted their construct dimensions. The person who maintained himself as a shocking person may not have entertained any particular subsuming construction of his neighbors' construction systems such as would be required if he were to meet our criterion of role. He need only have observed his neighbors' reactions without trying to construe them as functioning within any system but his own. We have insisted that the term *role* be reserved for a course of activity which is played out in the light of one's construction of one or more other persons' construct systems. When one plays a *role*, he behaves according to what he believes another person thinks, not merely according to what the other person appears to approve or disapprove. One plays a *role* when he views another person as a construer. This, of course, is a restricted definition of the term. It is the definition specifically used in the psychology of personal constructs. The term is used much more broadly elsewhere.

It should be apparent at once that one's construction of his role must necessarily be validated in terms of the expectancies of the persons with respect to whom he construes his role. In this case, the ultimate validating criteria are themselves the operations of the construct systems which appear to govern our neighbors' behaviors. Our very definition of *role* commits us to this position.

We have attempted to state the general way in which group expectancies operate as validators of personal constructs, and to mention three special types of cases. The general way is the same as the way all psychologists validate their theoretical approaches — by checking predictions of people's behavior against their subsequently observed behavior. People's behavior is taken as validating evidence for a considerable variety of personal constructs. Since people's behavior is believed to be statable in terms of their expectancies, this is tantamount to saying that group expectancies operate as validators of personal constructs. We are saying, simply, that everyone uses this approach. The special cases are (1) the necessary acceptance of group judgments as validators of any construct for which more direct evidence is not available, (2) the implicit and inescapable acceptance of group expectancies as validators whenever one tries to maintain a pose, and (3) the acceptance, by definition, of group expectancy-governing constructs as validators of one's own *role constructs*. It is this last special case which is illustrative of the characteristic approach of the personal-construct psychologist to other people, for he, by his Fundamental Postulate, must seek validation of his understanding of other people by checking it against their personal construct systems. The personal-construct psychologist thus seeks to establish for himself a role in relation to other people. Personal-construct theory might have been called "role theory." In fact, this was the term by which it was known among the writer's students during the earlier stages of its development.

The psychology of personal constructs, rather than being a system in which the study of individual behavior leaves no place for the study of group participation, is one which keeps open vast areas of social relationships to be explored by adventurous psychologists. The concept of individual suggestibility need not be considered, as it once was, the sole basis for a social psychology. Within the present psychological system the phenomenal areas of traditionalism, social controls, law, cultural identification, and ethnic unity can properly be brought into the realm of psychology.

In this particular book the discussion of group expectancies as validators of personal constructs is preliminary to a discussion of what is believed to be one of the major areas of investigation in psychological clinical work: the analysis of the client's experience. It is hoped that it will serve to indicate that, while the theoretical point of view of the psychology of personal constructs is largely consonant with the ahistorical stand of perceptual theories, it is, in practice, very much concerned with the historical study of chronological elements upon which presently operating personal constructs are formed. It is particularly concerned with those chronological elements with respect to which the presently operating constructs cannot be directly elicited, in symbolic form or otherwise. The clinician must infer them by trying to form parallel constructs out of the same stuff.

22. GAINING ACCESS TO PERSONAL CONSTRUCTS THROUGH THE STUDY OF THE CULTURE IN WHICH THEY HAVE GROWN

In psychotherapeutic practice one never ceases to be impressed both by the differences in the problems of clients who come from different cultural backgrounds and by the similarities in the problems of clients who come from backgrounds which are similar. To be sure, these differences and similarities seem more crucial in diagnosis and the early stages of therapy.

Yet one cannot ignore them in establishing and maintaining an effective relationship with his client throughout the entire therapeutic series. As the therapeutic program moves along, the therapist more and more comes to see his client as an individual and thinks of him less and less as a member of a class. But the cultural identification is there to be seen whenever the therapist backs off and looks at it.

A failure to understand cultural controls may make the therapist insensitive to the disruptive nature of some of the client's anxieties. A few months ago the writer was supervising a therapy program in which the client was a Negro and the therapist was white. It was apparent that the client was avoiding the discussion of an extremely threatening topic, the nature of which was well enough perceived to enable him to skirt it consistently. After employing various techniques and assuring ourselves that the problem could probably be faced in the kind of therapeutic relationship already established, we put the client under a regime of physical tension during the interviews, and subjected him to a type of stress questioning ordinarily used only with the greatest of caution. At the third interview in this part of the series he told the therapist about his phantasies of intercourse with white women. His physical tension immediately became automatic; that is to say, he did not have to remind himself to keep his muscles tense or be reminded to do so by the therapist.

The client had discussed masturbation and sex phantasies before. The therapist, who was inexperienced in therapy with clients from this type of cultural background, had only one cue regarding the deeply disturbing nature of the material elicited; that was the motor behavior of the client. Fortunately, this was so marked that the therapist, who was fully alert to this kind of semeiotics in therapy, could not overlook the significance of the material associated with the change in behavior. (If the client had been under a physical-relaxation regime at the time the material was elicited, it would have been much easier to have overlooked its traumatic nature. The relationship between a tension set and the clear-cut and obvious revelation of the trau-

matic nature of the material elicited is appreciated by trial law-
yers who "break down" certain kinds of witnesses on the stand.)
The problem for this therapist, after the traumatic nature of the
material had been so clearly revealed, was to understand the
nature of the threat to the client's basic construct system. With
the help of another therapist, who was familiar with the client's
type of cultural background, it was possible to come to appre-
ciate the way in which cultural controls, especially those against
interracial sex behavior, operated in the client's group.

The client had been forced to construe the crosscurrents of
two different cultures. In his high school there were few other
colored students, and he had seen himself as more or less accepted by his white peers. His home, however, came wholly
under the control system of a Negro culture. His phantasies of
intercourse with white women threatened him with the loss of
his basic role and he experienced painful guilt feelings. It was
not surprising that he was, before and during the early period
of therapy, frantically engaging in group organizational activity
directed toward the improvement of the social status of his race.

There are other illustrations which can be cited to indicate
the access which can be obtained to personal constructs via a
study of cultural controls. The therapist who comes in contact
with a series of rural clients for the first time may be struck
and possibly baffled by their similarity. If he attempts to relate
the "run" of clients to his own diagnostic construct system, he
may come up with some such notion as "farmers tend to be
schizoid." This is stereotypy, not diagnosis!

The Gentile therapist who comes in contact with a series of
Jewish clients for the first time may also be baffled by the similarities he sees by way of contrast with his other clients. If he
is to understand them as persons, rather than to stereotype them
as Jews, he must neither ignore the cultural expectations under
which they have validated their constructs — expectation of both
Jewish and Gentile groups — nor make the mistake of focusing
on the group constructs to the exclusion of the personal constructs of each client. If he stops with group constructs, he does
an injustice to his clients; if he sees group constructs as the

elements upon which his clients must have had to form personal constructs about themselves and their companions, he may come to understand the obstacles and aspirations which play such an important part in their personal readjustment.

Moreover, the Gentile therapist who seeks to understand a Jewish client must have some appreciation of the family ties which are characteristic of the culture, and which the client must do something about, one way or another, if he is to develop a personal construct system enabling him to get along in the world. This is not to say that the Jewish client, who thinks he needs to do so, cannot ever hope to differentiate himself from his family or from his culture; indeed, he may, if he considers it necessary, do an unusually decisive job of it. It means, rather, that if he does the job, he will have to have a formula for it, a construct or system of constructs which will permit him to see the surrounding contrary expectations as not necessarily invalidating his construct of independence. It may take a while to work out his formula for release, and he may apply it in a number of inappropriate forms before he gets the "bugs out of it," but eventually there is no reason why he cannot be just as free of cultural conventionality as his capacity for forming new ideas will permit him to be. Indeed, in a sense, he may become more free — for his new personal construct may give him a clearly constructed path leading elsewhere.

What we have said with respect to a client's adjustment to his Jewish cultural background is equally applicable to any client's adjustment to any cultural system similarly well integrated. One does not escape from his cultural controls (assuming that there is ever any reason to escape) simply by ignoring them — he must *construe* his way out. Some people try to *fight* their way out by being perverse; but they, as we have already suggested, often end up by being more than ever like the persons whom they have rejected. Others concern themselves less with the problem of extrication and approach the matter from the standpoint of overriding principles. They are likely to be happier with their results.

There is much more to be said about man's experiences and actions within the framework of our culture. But it can wait. For now it is sufficient to illustrate the broader implications of personal construing. Perhaps it is clear enough that personal constructs are the tools of experience rather than its products merely.

23. CONCLUSION

Thus begins a story. The psychology of personal constructs is not so much a theory about man as it is a theory of man. Certainly this is no treatise to be studied by one who prefers to be disidentified with the human race. It is, rather, part of a psychologist's protracted effort to catch the sense of man going about his business of being human, and what on earth it means to be a person. Howsoever forces are seen to press upon this creature — this man — this person — or what manner of surroundings are said to make decisive demands upon his actions, or even which conjured motives are presumed to drive the biological organism; these are all topics of another style of discipline — also called "psychology" — and they have no place in this discourse.

Our theme is the personal adventure of the men we are and live with — the efforts, the enterprises, the ontology of individuals so convinced there is something out there, really and truly, that they will not relent, no matter what befalls them, until they have seized it in their own hands. Moreover, nothing in this psychology we envision precludes verification or foredooms our efforts to the vagueness so often associated with attempts to understand the inner man. In simplest terms this is a disciplined psychology of the inner outlook, a psychology that is, on the one hand, an unabashed alternative to the scientistic psychologies of the outer inlook, and, on the other, a calculated step beyond the experiential psychologies of inner *inner* feelings.

Bibliography

1. Adler, A. *The practice and theory of individual psychology.* New York: Harcourt, 1927.
2. Allport, G. W. *Personality: A psychological interpretation.* New York: Holt, 1937.
3. Bieri, James. A study of generalization of changes within the personal construct system. Unpub. Ph.D. dissertation, Ohio State Univ., 1953.
4. Bridgman, P. W. *The way things are.* Cambridge: Harvard Univ. Press, 1959.
5. Bugental, J. F. T. A method for assessing self and not-self attitudes during the therapeutic series. *J. consult. Psychol.,* 1952, *16,* 435–439.
6. Dewey, John. *How we think.* Boston: Heath, 1910.
7. Freud, Sigmund. *New introductory lectures on psychoanalysis.* New York: Norton, 1933.
8. Howard, A. R. and Kelly, G. A. A theoretical approach to psychological movement. *J. abnorm. soc. Psychol.,* 1954, *49,* 399–404.
9. Hull, C. L. *Principles of behavior.* New York: Appleton-Century-Crofts, 1943.
10. Landfield, A. W. A movement interpretation of threat. *J. abnorm. soc. Psychol.,* 1954, *49,* 529–532.
11. Lecky, Prescott. *Self-consistency: A theory of personality.* New York: Long Island Press, 1945.
12. Lyle, W. H. A comparison of emergence and value as determinants of selective perception. Uupub. Ph.D. dissertation, Ohio State Univ., 1953.
13. McGaughran, L. S. Predicting language behavior from object sorting. *J. abnorm. soc. Psychol.,* 1954, *49,* 183–195.
14. Murray, H. W. *Manual of thematic apperception test.* Cambridge: Harvard Univ. Press, 1943.

15. Poch, Susanne M. A study of changes in personal constructs as related to interpersonal prediction and its outcome. Unpub. Ph.D. dissertation, Ohio State Univ., 1952.

16. Raimy, V. C. Self reference in counseling interviews. *J. consult. Psychol.*, 1948, *12*, 153–163.

17. Rogers, C. R. *Client-centered therapy*. Boston: Houghton-Mifflin, 1951.

18. Snygg, Donald and A. W. Combs. *Individual Behavior* (Rev. ed.). New York: Harper, 1959.

19. Stern, William. *General psychology from the personalistic standpoint* (trans. by H. D. Spoerl). New York: Macmillan, 1938.

20. Sullivan, H. S. *The interpersonal theory of psychiatry*. New York: Norton, 1953.

21. Vygotsky (alt. Vigotsky), L. S. *Thought and language* (Ed. and trans. by Eugenia Hanfmann and Gertrude Vakar). New York: Wiley, 1962.

Index

Author Index

CPSIA information can be obtained at www.ICGtesting.com
Printed in the USA
LVOW11s1716070116

469593LV00001B/7/P